New & Updated

Posh &
Becks
"Talking"

OMNIBUS PRESS

POSH & BECKS *Talking*

Copyright © 2002 Omnibus Press
(A Division of Music Sales Limited)

Cover & Book designed by Phil Gambrill @ Fresh Lemon.
Picture research by Nikki Lloyd & Steve Behan.

ISBN: 0.7119.9643.1
Order No: OP49214

Exclusive Distributors:
Music Sales Limited,
8/9 Frith Street, London W1D 3JB, UK.

Music Sales Corporation,
257 Park Avenue South, New York, NY 10010, USA.

Macmillan Distribution Services,
53 Park West Drive, Derrimut, Vic 3030, Australia.

To the Music Trade only:
Music Sales Limited,
8/9 Frith Street, London W1D 3JB, UK.

Photo credits:
Front cover: Rex Features; Back cover: LFI.
All other pictures supplied by PA Photos, Camera Press,
Big Pictures, LFI & Rex Features.

Every effort has been made to trace the copyright holders of the
photographs in this book but one or two were unreachable.
We would be grateful if the photographers concerned would contact us.

Printed by: Caligraving Limited, Thetford, Norfolk.

A catalogue record for this book is available from the British Library.

Visit Omnibus Press on the web at www.omnibuspress.com

CONTENTS

My grateful thanks and appreciation goes to the
following publications/TV companies for providing source material:
BBC, Big!, Daily Express, Daily Mail, Daily Star, Daily Telegraph,
Entertainment Weekly, Esquire, GMTV, Hello!, ITN, News Of The World, Q,
Sky One, Sky Sports, Sunday Mirror, Sunday Sport, The Sun,
Time Out, Just Seventeen, Live And Kicking Magazine, Marie Claire, Metro,
Ms. London, Now, OK! Sunday Express, Sunday Telegraph, The Guardian,
The Independent, The Mirror, The Tatler, Vogue.

Particular thanks to Heat (the bible of all things Posh & Becks),
The Michael Parkinson Show, There's Only One David Beckham
and the inimitable Chris Charlesworth.

I must also express all due appreciation to the following websites:
www.angelfire.com, The Spice & Geri Net, gurl.com/gurlpages,
BBC News, BBC Sport, Nuthin' But Spice, Picture Perfect Posh,
virgin.net and Virtual Manchester

All thanks to those whose views are included in this book, and of course,
a king big thank you to David and Victoria Beckham themselves.

ACKNOWLEDGEMENTS ,,

If you pitched the story of 'Posh & Becks' to a fiction editor,
he'd laugh you out the door. After all, the concept is preposterous.
Take England's, perhaps the world's most talented footballer.
Have him marry a member of the most popular female group of all
time. Throw in a cute little baby boy. Then move the family into
a fairytale palace, where they all live happily ever after.
Doesn't sound particularly realistic, does it?

Introduction

Nonetheless, the story of David and Victoria Beckham moves
precisely along such improbable lines. He is "Golden Balls", captain
of the national team and Manchester United's most valuable asset.
She is "Easy V... a real lady", who as a member of The Spice Girls,
found unprecedented levels of stardom throughout the Nineties and
beyond. Together, they are 'Posh & Becks', Great Britain's most
recognisable celebrity couple, and according to Fleet Street at least,
"the *real* King and Queen of England."

David And Victoria Beckham: In Their Own Words charts the meteoric
rise of 'Posh & Becks', from their vastly different childhoods to the
international playgrounds of football and pop music. From their first
meeting at Manchester United's Old Trafford ground in late 1997 to
their spectacular wedding ceremony in July, 1999. Brooklyn, fashion,
free kicks and red cards - it's all here. A unique tale, with a
distinguished celebrity cast, the story of David and Victoria is one of

personal loss and spectacular gain lived out beneath the
unforgiving glare of the camera lens. Above all though,
it's a story of love and *true* romance...

Chapter One

Footer & Dancing

DAVID AND VICTORIA ON SCHOOLDAYS, APPRENTICESHIPS, PLAYGROUND BULLIES AND CLOCKWORK BALLERINAS...

DAVID

"My mum and dad are the reason I'm the person I am today. They got me here. Yes, I worked hard, but they're the reason."

"When I was a kid, I lived for the game. The football was the first thing I got out when I got up and the last thing I put away before I went to bed. I just couldn't get enough... it didn't matter to me whether it was Wembley Stadium or a piece of parkland near our home in Chingford."

"As a kid, I used to run around my local park pretending I was Manchester United skipper, Bryan Robson, scoring goals. He was my idol."

"I would play football on my own for hours – or else with my dad... all my dad and I talk about is football!"

"When I was young, my dad always used to encourage my football. That's something I'll try and do with my own son, should he wish it."

POSH & **BECKS** *Talking*

"Even as a boy, I always tried to strike the ball properly. I have seen videos of me when I was six or seven doing just that."

"When I was young, I used to whack the free kicks. They'd go over the keepers' heads because they were so little."

"I've always had willpower. And I've always said that when my mates were down the road, standing on the corner drinking cider, I was at home watching *Match Of The Day*."

"Nothing ever distracted me from my football."

"Running has always been part of me. I was 1,500 metres Champion at school for four years on the trot, and I used to do cross-country competitions which I loved. In fact, I used to get more nervous doing those runs than I ever do playing in front of 50,000 people."

"If you stuck a girl or a ball in front of David he'd pick up the ball."

JOHN BULLOCK, DAVID'S
SPORTS TEACHER

"I think it's important to remove the idea that football is an exclusively male domain. When I was at school, some of the girls were as good as the boys. Getting girls involved might help to remove some of the macho nonsense that mars the game."

"Loads of kids want to become professional footballers and you just can't blame them. (You're) in the fantastic position of being able to say 'My job is my hobby'"

"I don't know what I would have done if I didn't have football. I always enjoyed drawing, so maybe I'd something in art. But football was always number one."

"I dreamt a lot about football and a lot of those dreams came true for me.**"**

"My mum and dad gave me all the advice I needed. But in the end, they left the big decision up to me – whether it was to (apprentice) with Manchester United, or to stay in London and play for Tottenham or Arsenal. They never said 'We support Manchester United, so you're going up there'. I think that was important, because if you're pushed into something, you go the other way."

"Signing that piece of paper was just brilliant.**"**
DAVID RECALLS THE MOMENT HE SIGNED AS A TRAINEE FOR MANCHESTER UNITED

FOOTER & DANCING

❝Sir Bobby Charlton said I was the best eleven year old he'd seen in the six years of running his school.❞

❝David Beckham was unusual. He was desperate to be a footballer. His mind was made up when he was nine or ten. Many kids think that it's beyond them. But you can't succeed without practising at any sport.❞ SIR BOBBY CHARLTON

❝My belief is practice makes perfect. If I didn't practice, I suppose I wouldn't be able to put the ball on a sixpence as often as I do. When you don't get it right, you just have to practice some more...❞

❝From day one, his talent had to be seen to be believed.❞
MANCHESTER UNITED YOUTH COACH, ERIC HARRISON

❝I know when the ball was going in. I was always able to hit them like that, even as a kid. But I used to practice them back then too. That's why they come off.❞
David on the art of free kicks.

❝When I came up to Manchester I stayed in the halls of residence and played football every single day for two weeks. It was my idea of heaven.❞

❝I watched David Beckham develop at Manchester United, and none of the senior players had any doubt about how big he would be. Now his reputation precedes him.❞
FORMER MANCHESTER UNITED
CAPTAIN BRYAN ROBSON

"We used to bring David to our games in London. He was our mascot at West Ham when he was only twelve."

MANCHESTER UNITED MANAGER ALEX FERGUSON

"I couldn't get enough of United as a kid, I knew it was the club for me."

"The opportunities are even better now than when I was a kid. But if you don't enjoy your football you can have the best facilities in the world and it doesn't count for anything."

"I never refuse to sign an autograph, because I know how I felt as a kid when I was turned down."

"My ambition is to stay at Manchester United, become captain and be the best player in the world..."

VICTORIA

"My dad was in a band in the Sixties. He wanted to be famous and all the rest of it."

"My dad's self-made. He worked very hard for everything he's got."

"I've always dreamed of being famous, ever since childhood."

"My childhood was comfortable, but my brother, sister and I were never spoilt."

"I had three dogs. Lucy, a Yorkshire Terrier. Bambi, a Yorkshire terrier and Tiger, who again,is a Yorkshire Terrier. But I actually wanted to buy a goldfish!"

"I was always very well behaved at school..."

FOOTER & DANCING

"Victoria was always a pleasant child, very pretty – not at all loud or pushy. She always worked hard and came from a lovely family. I remember her in the leading role of the 'Pied Piper'. She was always in school productions... very keen on drama."

SUSAN BAILEY, ONE OF VICTORIA'S TEACHERS AT GOFF'S OAK SCHOOL

"I've been dancing since the age of three. I trained at theatre school."

"I used to get on with my work. I used to be at school on time. I wasn't round the back of the sheds having a fag or drinking or having loads of boyfriends. I didn't even have a boy friend. I was really well behaved and that isn't the cool thing to be. I was just totally straight."

"When I was younger, I occasionally lied and said I was ill so I could skip school."

"Victoria had a bad time at senior school. They didn't like her because she didn't go out every night and hang around on street corners. Instead, she used to go to singing and dancing lessons." VICTORIA'S SISTER, LOUISE ADAMS

"When everybody else was having boyfriends and going to parties, I was at ballet class. I didn't really have a lot of friends, and I was never a rebel. I was never particularly intelligent. I was a nice kid, that's the bottom line, and I worked hard."

"I was one of the most unpopular kids (at school). I was a complete wreck... very paranoid about everything. I would wake up worrying who I was going to sit next to in class. It was sheer hell."

"I didn't even have a nickname at school because nobody would talk to me."

"Children can be awfully cruel sometimes. When I was growing up, I was the victim of some really nasty bullying."

"My heart goes out to anyone who's been bullied, because children can be so cruel – physically and mentally. I get a lot of letters from fans saying they are bullied and it breaks my heart reading them. I wish I could do more to help."

"The best revenge is to be strong. When you grow up, you find out being different is a good thing..."

"I wasn't a stunning teenager. I was bullied a t school because I had bad skin, so I wasn't confident about the way I looked back then. At the time, all I wanted to do was to work hard and do my best, but that wasn't deemed cool by the rest of my class. I never had any real friends. It was a horrible period of my life, but I did have my family to support me."

"My mum and dad always kept me grounded. They never treated me differently from my brother and sister."

"I remember saying to my teachers at school: 'I really want to be a dancer'. They just said: 'C'mon, what do you really want to do?'"

"In the end, I got good grades at school. And I always worked very hard... I think it's important to get good qualifications, even if you want a more artistic job."

"I was always the underdog – never one of the pretty girls or the best singer or dancer. Even at school, I was the last to finish *Janet And John*. But I'm proof that if you want something enough, you *can* get it."

"When I was younger, people tried to pressurise me into sex and I wouldn't do it. I've always had a strong personality and if I don't want to do something, no one can make me do it.

Too many people think because all their friends are doing it, they should too. But everybody should make up their own minds about it. "

" My first job was a dancer in a musical. It was called *Bertie*, and I was a clockwork ballerina! **"**

"When I was a kid, I was... told I'd never be good at anything. But I had a really strong personality. Believe in yourself, and who has the last laugh? "

" I'm one of these people who, when someone kicks them, tries hard to get up again. **"**

VICTORIA AND SISTER LOUISE

FOOTER & **DANCING** "

Chapter Two

3 Lions & A Red Devil

FOOTBALL, FOOTBALL & FOOTBALLER'S WIVES...

David Beckham's thoughts on playing for Manchester United, his team mates, footballing tactics and the will to win...

"The current Manchester United side has grown up together as friends. We trust each other and that comes out on and off the field. All the players who have joined the side over the years have slotted into that unit and created a togetherness."

"Gary Neville's my best friend. Out of all the Manchester United players, I get on best with him. We socialise a lot. To be honest, I think he's one of England's, no... Europe's, no... the world's best right backs. I'm not just saying that because he's my mate, but because I personally think he's a great player."

"When David wants you to kick the ball he yells "It it', which sounds really funny. Then when you get into the back of his car, he says 'Don't scuff me levver'. We're always imitating him, but he doesn't mind. He just laughs." MANCHESTER UNITED TEAMATE RYAN GIGGS

"Ryan's a very easy going bloke. And what a great player!"

POSH & **BECKS** *Talking*

"Our captain, Roy Keane, is quite mischievous. He can play a few jokes on you. He's a very funny bloke with a dry sense of humour. He can say things and you just crease up. Great bloke."

"Andy Cole's an excellent finisher and an asset to Manchester United. Off the pitch, he's a friendly fella too, with a nice Cockney sense of humour."

"It's like Christmas coming every Saturday."
                    MANCHESTER UNITED STRIKER ANDY COLE ON DAVID'S PASSING ABILITY

"If we work hard, then the manager can't ask for much more. When every player on the pitch works hard, you are going to get a break in the end."

"I think I can do as much with my career with Manchester United as would be possible with any foreign club. With the trophies you get here, it's enough for any player to ask for. I think I can get all the satisfaction from (Manchester United) that I need... I don't need to look elsewhere."

"Every new season is big for me. I go into each one wanting to win everything."

"It's always important for us to get our first game out of the way with a win."

"A win is a win. The win is all important."

"I love scoring goals, especially important ones. A lot of the time they go to other players, so it's nice to score goals... and get an ovation."

"If we keep going, we'll get our just desserts."
DAVID ON MANCHESTER UNITED'S WINNING STRATEGY

"I won the Double at 21 years old and that's unbelievable. But it didn't just doesn't end there."

"Manchester United... The Heroes Who United A Nation."
THE DAILY MAIL

"Records are made to be broken."
DAVID'S COMMENT AFTER MANCHESTER UNITED WON A UNIQUE TREBLE ON MAY 26TH, 1999

"Tackling is my weakest point. I've never been good at it. I'm always late or I mistime it."

"I'm quite a confident person, but I do get nervous. Then... I relax."

"I get a bit annoyed when it's said I can't use my left foot. Most players can only stand on theirs. Mine's a bit better than that."

"David's a really fine player in every respect. He has 'two feet' which a lot of people say players don't have these days."
SOCCER PUNDIT JIMMY HILL

"My nan loves to watch me on TV, but is always saying how often I seem to argue with referees. Worse than that is the fact that my nan is an excellent lip-reader. She knows exactly what I'm saying."

"It's nice to see boys and girls walking down the street with 'Beckham' shirts and the number seven on their back. It makes me smile when I see that."

3 LIONS & **A RED DEVIL**

"He's one of the lads. Kevin Keegan. You know where you stand with him. Instead of sitting at the front of the coach, he'll sit with the lads."

"David is the best crosser of a ball in Europe. The best striker of a dead ball I have *ever* come across. He's totally outstanding."

**MANCHESTER UNITED MANAGER
SIR ALEX FERGUSON**

SIR ALEX FERGUSON

David on his relationship with Sir Alex...

"I would like to stay in the game when I eventually finish playing, but I don't think I'd fancy management. There's just too much hassle..."

"From the first day I came to the club Sir Alex has been like a father figure to me. He's been exactly what any player would need. Someone to look up to. He's also told me when I've done things right, and when I've done things wrong. Most importantly, he has given me the confidence to become the player I am. Obviously, everyone can have an occasional disagreement with his boss, and I've had one or two since I've been at the club."

"The fact is when I've had the odd disagreement with Sir Alex, it's been made into a crisis by the papers because it's me. But we've always got on and there's never been any real problem."

"It doesn't matter how high a player's profile is. If he is in the wrong, he is in the wrong, and David was definitely in the wrong. Nicky Butt, Phil Neville and Ole Gunnar

Solskaer cannot count on being regulars in the first team, but they are model players who never miss training. (It was not) a satisfactory reason for being absent. **"**

**SIR ALEX ON TEMPORARILY DROPPING DAVID FROM
THE MANCHESTER UNITED TEAM WHEN HE MISSED TRAINING.
ACCORDING TO BECKHAM, HIS SON, BROOKLYN, WAS ILL AND NEEDED HIS FATHER**

**"The papers are a danger for David. I try to protect him...
make him stay down to earth. Or else."** SIR ALEX FERGUSON

JERRY SPRINGER: **"**If you could save either Sir Alex Ferguson or Geri Halliwell from a sinking ship, who would it be?**"**
VICTORIA: **"**Neither. I'd just sail off and let them both drown...**"**

"Victoria, no matter one anyone says, has got a great relationship with Sir Alex. There's never been an problem."

"All my impressions of Sir Alex Ferguson are that he's a nice man and he's really good at his job. But I don't think he realises that when he says (he has) problems with David, it's me who has to put up with the negativity.**"**

3 LIONS & A RED DEVIL

POSH & **BECKS** *Talking*

"The players know I don't hold any grudges. I haven't got time to hold any grudges."

"What do I call him? Sir..." DAVID BECKHAM ON HIS MANAGER

David on his England captaincy and World Cup 2002...

"What has playing for Manchester United got to do with playing for your country?"

"I dream of playing in the centre for England. That's where I think I can give my best. I'm dream of playing in Paul Gascoigne's spot and to see my soccer have as much effect on the national team as Paul's did."

"Achieving what I have at Manchester United has been amazing, but winning something with England can only add to it. But I've still got a lot to learn at international level as well as at club level."

DAVID WITH FELLOW ENGLAND PLAYERS MICHAEL OWEN AND DAVID SEAMEN

"Obviously I'd like to score more goals for England. Who wouldn't?**"**

"Inevitably, there are confrontations that take place from week to week with club sides, but you can't afford to hang on to them when you arrive in the national team."

"I looked for the best player in the squad to captain the England team, and there was only one choice: David Beckham. The way he handled himself, especially after the Argentina game was superb. He demonstrated how strong a character he was. I said to him: 'I'm making you skipper', and I don't think I gave him the option of turning it down.**" ENGLAND COACH, PETER TAYLOR**

"I got the phone call one morning from Peter Taylor to tell me I was captain of the full squad. It took a minute or so or it to sink in. Everyone knows what happened three years ago, so to come through it like that was great."

"I was so proud of David. It was amazing when we found out he was going to be England captain. I'll always support him in everything he does.**" VICTORIA**

"I was very nervous the first time I was made England captain. Everyone said I wasn't up to the job. Obviously, I had a lot to prove. But whatever people throw at me, I'll keep trying to make them think again. Now, I want to stay England captain for the rest of my career. I don't want to play for my country again and not wear that armband - I love the responsibility. Being England skipper is an unbelievable feeling, the best I've ever had in football. When you've done the job once, you never want to let it go..."

"David Beckham is respected by the coaches, the manager and his team-mates. I would be surprised if the job of England captain went to anyone else in the next few years.**"**

FORMER ENGLAND COACH, PETER TAYLOR

3 LIONS & **A RED DEVIL**

"I'd never ever been a senior captain before – apart from one game at Manchester united when no-one wanted to do it."

"David Beckham can make a good England captain. More than anything else, you need the respect of your fellow team-mates, and he certainly has that. Some lead by grabbing people by the scruff of the neck, and giving them a good kick up the backside. Others can be just as good with a well-chosen word here and there. Perhaps (David) will lead by example, scoring a good goal, making a crucial tackle, passing a great ball. You influence people by what you do on the pitch." **FORMER ENGLAND CAPTAIN TERRY BUTCHER**

"To be made captain of the England team when we're doing so well is one of the greatest honours I could have been given in football."

"David doesn't waste energy. You don't see him ducking or diving or throwing tantrums like some wingers. He whips the ball in first time. That means he doesn't waste energy going past his man."
FORMER ENGLAND MANAGER, KEVIN KEEGAN

"It's a challenge to play football against the best players in the world. And it's also a chance to stake a claim for myself."

"Everyone knows how well England are doing. Manchester United must do the same"

"I think he was a very good choice for England captain. I also think maybe he's the most famous footballer in England... perhaps even the world. Every football fan knows who David Beckham is. He sets a very good example, and so far, has done very, very well. I hope it's going to be for a long time."
CURRENT ENGLAND COACH, SVEN GORAN ERIKSSON

"Sven Goran Eriksson is such a calm man, such a calming influence. The players are so relaxed around him."

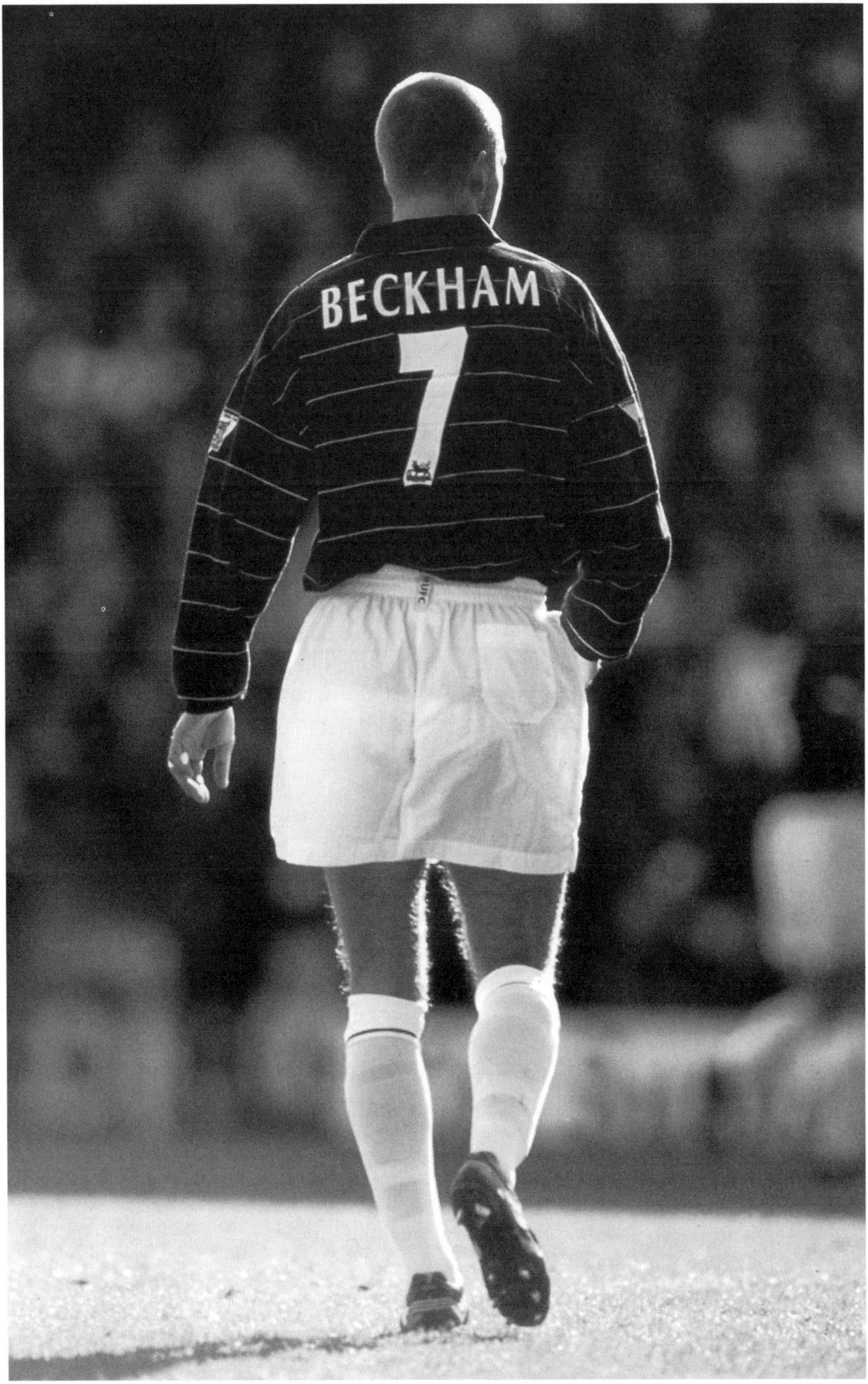
BECKHAM
7

"We've reached a stage where we're in with a real chance of going to the World Cup and not being scared of anyone – not even the French. After beating Germany 5-1, we don't have to worry about any other country. Believe me, there's a lot more to come from this team."

"I'll be a failure if I don't lift a trophy as England captain. Success with the national team is an absolute must."

"People have said 2002 is too early for the England team to go to the World Cup and do really well. I don't agree. I've had success all the way with Manchester United and that feeling is immense. Now I have to bring that to this England team."

"When you follow David's career in the papers, you read a lot about his wife and so on, but you don't really get to know him as a person. And I must say David is a big, big professional, a big, big captain. He's shown that by his performances." SVEN GORAN ERIKSSON

DAVID WITH ENGLAND TEAM-MATES RIO FERDINAND, DAVID SEAMEN, ALAN SHEARER AND MICHAEL OWEN

❝I want youngsters to look up to me and copy the things I do on the pitch for England and United. The most important I learned in the early days was to enjoy my football, and that's what I'm trying to pass on to kids today.❞

❝We've all dreamed of winning the World Cup, and I'm no different to anyone else...❞

Footballers old and new offer their opinion on David's gift...

❝David Beckham works harder than any footballer I've ever seen on a pitch. He never gives up.❞ GEORGE BEST

❝There's so much more to David Beckham than we've seen so far.❞
KEVIN KEEGAN

3 LIONS & A RED DEVIL ❞

"David must take it as a compliment that other teams close him down so much. They do it because they fear him."

BRYAN ROBSON

"He can put a ball on someone's head from fifty yards.**"**

PAUL MERSON

"There's not many people who work as hard as David Beckham."

MICHAEL OWEN

"David Beckham has won the respect and admiration of everyone because of the way he has conducted himself on and off the pitch. Everybody loves him and so they should. But the transformation (since World Cup '98) is in the way the country thinks about him is solely down to him. David Beckham really is 'King Becks'.**"**

ENGLAND/LEEDS GOALKEEPER NIGEL MARTYN

"I don't think you realise quite how good he is until you play alongside him. He can do so many things with a football. He's got the world at his feet." ALAN SHEARER

"David Beckham has been a brilliant role model for me. He has grown in stature since becoming captain and made life easier for all the young players in the England squad.**"**

ENGLAND FULL-BACK ASHLEY COLE

"David Beckham is a suitable role model for every starry-eyed kid in the land." *THE SUN*

"Obviously, it's nice for people to talk like that, but if I listen too much, I start worrying. I just have to switch off from all the fame and acclaim... I have to focus on not getting big headed about it. Obviously, there is praise and adulation, but it's all about keeping my feet on the ground and having good people around me.**"**

And finally, Victoria's views on a national obsession...

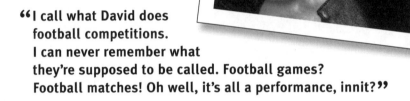

"You might not like the team David plays for, but you can't dispute the fact he's a fantastic footballer."

"There aren't any other footballers I particularly fancy. I've got the best one, haven't I?"

"I call what David does football competitions. I can never remember what they're supposed to be called. Football games? Football matches! Oh well, it's all a performance, innit?"

"I don't think Victoria knows about the off-side rule..." **DAVID**

"I know what a goal is, which is surely the most important thing in football, but I don't know about the offside rule, or stuff like that."

"I'm not the football wife type. I don't even know the rules of football."

"Actually, some footballer's wives are really intelligent. A lot of them have degrees. I suppose you might get one or two who might be a bit divvy, but it's the same in every walk of life."

"I'm not a football fan, but I like to watch David. But I'd be bored to death if I had to watch a game and he wasn't playing in it."

"I like David for him, and I don't care what he does as long as it makes him happy."

3 LIONS & A RED DEVIL

Chapter Three

Five Girls Take On The World. And Win.

VICTORIA AND THE SPICE GIRLS ON THEIR BEGINNINGS, GLOBAL DOMINATION, THE GINGER ONE AND THE FUTURE...

"The Spice girls? We were always the crap ones left behind at auditions..." **VICTORIA**

"We moved into a house together, began writing our own material and started our own 'Spicy' mission." VICTORIA

"We'd all known each other (before the Spice Girls) for different amounts of time. I became friends with Emma when I was nine years old." **VICTORIA**

"(The house we lived in) had two bedrooms and one very, very small bedroom... more like a cupboard, actually. Geri lived in the 'cupboard' because she was the oldest. I shared a room with Emma." VICTORIA

"Once you meet us, you realise we're normal. Whatever normal is..." **GERI**

"Well... we were all mad to start off with!" MEL B

POSH & **BECKS** *Talking*

❝When I first met The Spice Girls, they used to leap on tables and dance about. I was the one who said 'I don't know if you should do that… the table might collapse.❞

VICTORIA

❝**A couple of us may be quiet while the rest of us are being loud. We give each other room.**❞ EMMA

❝It's just having a little bit of naughtiness inside you which makes you feel free. We don't do mad things for the sake of it, or to be nasty. We're just want to have fun!❞ GERI

❝**When we were in Japan, we found out we'd gone to Number One (in the UK). We ended up doing karaoke and teaching the Japanese people loads of silly dance moves. It was a quiet night for us!**❞ MEL C

❝We had a party in our hotel room… and persuaded this guy to do a striptease for us. He ended up starkers behind the curtains and we threw all his clothes out the window!❞ **EMMA**

❝**Yeah, we have our ups and downs, but we still have a giggle!**❞

MEL C

❝Being in a gang does boost your confidence…❞ **VICTORIA**

❝**I think the new lass has been around for a long time. Some guys mistake it for being too loud, or a bit tarty and up-front, and they can be afraid of it because they're getting a taste of their own medicine. They've treated us like little girls, and now it's time to fight back!**❞ MEL B

❝I was engaged to a bloke, but broke it off when I joined the Spice Girls. They helped me realise he wasn't right for me.❞ **VICTORIA**

"We're normal looking girls. None of us is six feet tall or skinny or flawless. There are girls who you never see with a double chin or looking ugly. We're saying, 'You don't have to look that way'. Nowadays, I think if you've got a fat bum, its great! So long as you love your fat bum. Besides, it's something to get a hold of, isn't it?" VICTORIA

"The difference was we wrote our all the material. We didn't all dress the same. We weren't afraid to sound controversial. We were just the way we were." **VICTORIA**

"We wanted to be a household name... like Fairy Liquid or Ajax."
VICTORIA

"We didn't choose our names, Sporty, Posh, Baby, Ginger. We were just given them by a UK teen magazine. But they just happened to fit perfectly." **VICTORIA**

"How do you become a Spice Girl? There are millions of Spice girls out there! It's all about positive attitude, having fun and doing what you want to do." VICTORIA

"The phrase 'Zig-a-zig-ah' (from 'Wannabe') means whatever you want it to mean. A kiss, a cuddle... use your imagination!"
VICTORIA

❝Ever since the first single, 'Wannabe', the song that broke us into the world of pop, people have been saying 'Oh, that's the end of them, they're a one hit wonder'. I suppose we'll have to deal with that all the way through our career.❞ MEL C

❝You could never dream of what's happened to us. It's a bit out of the ordinary.❞ **VICTORIA**

❝(We all) want to write, everybody wants to have a go at singing. Everyone has an opinion. We have flaming rows about tiny things,bits of words we want to put in lyrically. But right from day one we've had an American attitude. If something's wrong, we're just open about it. It sounds disgustingly sick, but we're more like sisters than anything else.❞ VICTORIA

❝Of course you're going to have arguments. You're going to have disagreements. But that's only natural when you have five girls all living together.❞ **VICTORIA**

❝What The Spice Girls have got going is a kind of boyfriend/girlfriend relationship. We're very close and brutally honest with each other. We learn off each other. It's the best way to be.❞ MEL B

❝From the very beginning, we really managed ourselves. We've always had control of our lives. And we're not going to let that go.❞ MEL C

❝This is still a male dominated industry. A lot of people think there's some bloke behind the scenes who writes all the songs. But we've written all our own songs. People still don't like to believe that.❞ VICTORIA

"We've had some really rough times getting here, so when we do taste the high life and hear the kids screaming, we really appreciate it." **VICTORIA**

"We have the best fans. We've never had a show where they're dead!" EMMA

"The only people who care about The Spice Girls are four-year-old kids. Their music is nothing." **OASIS' LIAM GALLAGHER**

"Oasis? They say they're bigger than God? What does that make us then? Bigger than Buddha? Because we're a damn sight bigger than Oasis..." MEL C

"Onstage, I have to pretend to be the cool Spice Girl, and I find it really hard to look so miserable! I look really bored, but the fans seem to love it. All the other girls are working really hard, running about and kicking their legs, and there I am – just standing there and not doing any work!" **VICTORIA**

"The fans are the best critics. They'll either tell us if we're great or if we're rubbish. They're controlling our destiny." GERI

"Sometimes, it can be quite lonely on tour... being on your own. So it's good to have all your friends in the band around you."
VICTORIA

"How do I cope with homesickness? I just have a breakdown and cry a lot..." VICTORIA

"We're really busy all the time and away from home way too much. But I get 30% off Gucci now, which is key!" **VICTORIA**

"If nobody liked The Spice Girls, we'd still be doing this for ourselves. In the end, I'm doing this to make myself and these four happy." VICTORIA

FIVE GIRLS TAKE ON THE WORLD. AND WIN

"There's no room for complacency in The Spice Girls. We've got a lot to live up to." **VICTORIA**

"We don't want to be sexy. We don't want to put it up there. We want girls to relate to us." VICTORIA

"Everybody tries to 'sex' me up, but it just doesn't work. Victoria's very sexy, but not me." **EMMA**

"Emma's messy. Her room always looks like a hurricane hit it, and she's really tired and grumpy in the mornings..." VICTORIA

"You know, I'm always going to be known as 'Baby Spice', even when I'm 30!" **EMMA**

"You love it really, Emma. You always play up to it..." VICTORIA

"Victoria's a big spender, but tight with The Spice Girls! I mean, she buys all these designer outfits, but she wouldn't even buy us a drink!" **MEL B**

"There's just no room for bitchiness in this group..." VICTORIA

"If I want a cuddle or a cry, I'll go to Emma. If I fancy a wild night out, I'll go to Mel B, and if I want a good, honest answer, I'll go to Geri. And if I feel like a nice dinner, I'll go out with Mel C."

VICTORIA

"We went to this plush hotel in Hawaii and they didn't believe we were staying there. We were all in bikinis and bovver boots!"

GERI

"Sometimes I get annoyed because the others are a bit irrational. They just think of something and then do it. I will always think about the consequences..." **VICTORIA**

"I met Bryan Adams and screamed 'Come here, little boy!' slapped him on his bum and then sat him on my knee. I forgot he was this big megastar..." GERI

"We're up for anything!" MEL C

"When I want peace and quiet, I sit in the bath." VICTORIA

"The nastier you are to some creeps who try and chat you up, the more keen they get! It's better to ignore them... I used to get chatted up more *before* I was in the Spice Girls." VICTORIA

"Some blokes do think I'm a bit stand offish, so it's hard for me to get a guy. Unless, of course, I'm with Mel B. She goes straight over to whomever I fancy and chats them up for me! Embarrassing as that is, it certainly breaks the ice..." VICTORIA

"Am I a man-eater? I dunno. I have been one. We *all* have..." MEL B

"I was down the pub the other day, and I thought, 'If I didn't have a boyfriend, is there anyone here I'd like to talk to?' It was like, 'No!'

They're all standing there with their Ralph Lauren shirts on... a bit of fake tan... just like a uniform. I like a bit of individuality. VICTORIA

"With guys, I go for eye to eye contact, then I'll lunge. I chat 'em up with lines like 'Hey, Mr. Scorpio, here's 10p. Now go call your mum, because you're not going home tonight!" GERI

"At the 1995 Brit Awards, we were sitting next to Lenny Kravitz and Vanessa Paradis. They were serving all this posh food and Lenny said, 'I don't want to eat this!' So he pulled out this Jamaican takeaway and shared it with us. He's very sexy under his glasses." VICTORIA

"I really want to be Lenny Kravitz's rock chick!" EMMA

"We're not soul divas. We're just having a laugh." VICTORIA

"With us, it's 'What you see is what you get'. If you bumped into us in a supermarket, we'd just be our normal selves." EMMA

"People do look up to us, show us respect, but we're not quite ambassadors for Great Britain. I mean, we're proud to be British... sometimes." VICTORIA

"The people I enjoy meeting most are the fans. They're the ones who put us here. Most of the time, you're disillusioned when you meet famous people. Prince Charles was nice. He just wants to have fun. And I love Lady Diana..." VICTORIA

"Camilla Parker Bowles is just a old horse, isn't she?" VICTORIA

"We jabber on, but we're really not sure what they think we're saying. It's weird."

VICTORIA ON THE JOYS OF MEETING THE INTERNATIONAL PRESS

FIVE GIRLS TAKE ON THE WORLD. AND WIN

"In the past I've been asked by the press, 'If you were a piece of fruit, what piece of fruit would you be?' I just say, 'You what?'**"**

VICTORIA

"There's only one thing worse than bad press – no press!**"**

VICTORIA

In 1998, Geri Halliwell left the Spice Girls to launch a solo career. At first, it was all wine and roses:

"The Spice Girls are trying to express unity, to show how strong girls can be together. That's what we're all about – not trying to be stronger than blokes." GERI, 1996

"Being 'Ginger Spice' was a comfort zone. It was hard to walk out on all that. A bit like leaving a marriage." GERI, 1998

"There are no hard feelings. We wish her all the luck in the world and we're totally behind her. It was a shock to us... a complete shock, (but) the most important thing is our friendship. Fundamentally, we're friends.**" VICTORIA**

"We don't want her leaving to be nasty. What we've always said was that if Geri feels it's time to move on, we'll support her."

VICTORIA

"Good luck to her.**" MEL B**

Then things started to deteriorate:

"I didn't know we 'ad to come as Tank Girl, did I?"
GERI HALLIWELL RECALLS THE FIRST WORDS VICTORIA EVER SPOKE TO HER AT THE AUDITIONS FOR THE *TANK GIRL* MOVIE IN 1994

I didn't know Geri was leaving The Spice Girls, so I couldn't talk her out of it. In fact, I didn't find out (she was leaving) until we were told she'd left... VICTORIA

Victoria took up most of it with her massive suitcases.
GERI ON SHARING A ROOM WITH HER POSH FRIEND

Victoria, who had been in a band before, automatically assumed she was the lead singer and began dominating the vocals. GERI

Those hideous hair extensions. I don't know what Geri was doing, but it was vile. VICTORIA

For me, Geri's just cotton wool. She's not a talented musician and not a very strong singer. She's a great celebrity, but musically, it doesn't come from the heart. It's just hollow. MEL C

FIVE GIRLS TAKE ON THE WORLD. AND WIN

"If there are any negative comments from the girls, I just think, 'Oh, they don't really mean it'. You know, people sometimes say things when they're feeling emotional. Underneath of course, you think, 'That's not very nice', but we're all human. You could say something nasty about your sister or your friends, especially when they're getting on your nerves." GERI

"Geri left us totally in the lurch." VICTORIA

"I take my dog with me everywhere I go. Even to bed." GERI

"It's a power thing. Geri has a shih-tzu. I have two Dobermans." VICTORIA

"We've all tried to get I touch with her, but she doesn't return our calls. She can't seem to bring herself to talk to us." MEL C

"Geri was a very good friend to me, but things change. I don't speak to her now... it would be nice to see her and say 'Hi', but we don't have as much in common as we once did." VICTORIA

"The ball's in Geri's court now." MEL C

"She seems happy with herself, and I suppose that's the most important thing..." VICTORIA

The Spice Girls: Past, present and future...

"The press are always saying, 'That's it'. When we first arrived it was 'Five Girls? That'll never work'. But it did. Then, when we sacked our manager, it was, 'Well, that's the end of The Spice Girls'. It wasn't. Then Geri left and it was, 'A quartet? It'll never work'. 'Spice Girl pregnant?' Oh, shut up! I really don't believe people want to read all this negativity." VICTORIA

"We've been here years now and we're still here. We've just got the pleasure of going off and doing our own thing, and still being a rock solid band. I think people just can't comprehend that sometimes." MEL B

"The success of The Spice Girls hasn't quite sunk in yet. We were so busy working all the time, I don't think we had a chance to sit back and think about it." VICTORIA

"With The Spice Girls, we spent years on the road, recorded albums, recorded singles, did endless promotion. Now, I've got a family and a baby. I've got nothing to prove anymore..." VICTORIA

"Obviously, there are things we want to do individually as well as collectively." VICTORIA

"People are always saying we're going to split up, but we're going to be around for a long, long time." EMMA

"A lot of people think that everything The Spice Girls touched turned to gold, and that's how they think it's going to be for us individually. Yes, it happened for The Spice Girls, but life isn't always like that..." VICTORIA

Chapter Four

The Ballad Of Posh & Becks

DAVID AND VICTORIA RECOUNT THEIR FIRST MEETING, SUBSEQUENT ENGAGEMENT AND WEDDING IN JULY 1999...

"You know what? Everybody says 'You must have loads of blokes interested in you'. But I haven't..."

"My perfect man would have a sense of humour, a good pair of shoes and a healthy gold card."

"I first saw Victoria on the telly and I wanted to meet her. I knew I fancied her. So then it was just a case of getting together."

"He pointed at the TV and said 'That's the girl for me, and I'm going to get her.'"

DAVID'S BEST FRIEND, MANCHESTER UNITED'S GARY NEVILLE

"Actually, I fancied David long before I met him. I remember doing an interview with a magazine and they showed me photographs of loads of different footballers. I remember seeing David and thinking one word: 'Gorgeous'. I decided to stalk him."

POSH & **BECKS** *Talking*

"When we did first meet, I wanted to sound like I knew something about football. So I said something like, 'Good game then?' He just laughed, and that was it. I just knew."

"As soon as I met Victoria, I knew I was going to marry her. I had a sneaky feeling she might come to another game. I just couldn't stop thinking about her."

"I wasn't attracted by David's fame, but as we got to know each other, we realised it was a great bonus. We were equally famous."

"I liked Victoria for herself. I'd have liked her if she worked in Tesco."

"On our first date, we were thrown out of a Chinese restaurant in Chingford because neither of us wanted to eat. We'd gone there to find somewhere where we could have a quiet drink without being noticed. We actually ended in Mel C's flat."

"David was quite the groupie. After taking me out, he bought a Spice Girls CD to do some research."

"At first, David made no attempt to kiss me. But afterwards, he showered me with roses and a black Prada handbag. And I like a man who opens doors, takes me out to dinner and buys me flowers."

"I starting thinking about proposing marriage a week after I met her."

"I knew David liked me, but after three dates he still hadn't kissed me. He finally got round to it when we were at my parents' house. It was worth the wait."

"If you're a bloke, you go out and mess about with girls. It's (seen) as quite a cool thing to do. David has made it cool to be the opposite, really. You forever read about celebrities having affairs, but we're *not* like that."

"Before David Beckham, you thought of footballers as getting drunk, drinking beer... going out on the town. Not now."

LADY VICTORIA HERVEY

THE BALLAD OF POSH & BECKS

"At the start of our relationship, we were flying all over the place just to be with each other for an hour." **DAVID**

"**David is an animal in bed.**"

"I doubt when David wakes up next to me... he thinks he is lying next to one of the sexiest women in the world, because when I wake up I look shocking!"

"**I couldn't be happier. I've now got my dream woman.**"

"While I was in America, we decided we'd get engaged. I'd already told him what my dream ring would be, and he'd remembered and had it specially designed for me. So, we were sitting there in our pyjamas when David pulled out the ring, got down on one knee and said: 'Will you marry me, Victoria?' I said: 'Yes', then produced my own ring and said: 'Don't forget Girl Power... will you marry me?'"

"**David was everything I ever wanted in a person. We genuinely love each other. We're very good friends and very honest. I've found the man I going to get old and wrinkly with. Well, looks aren't going to last forever, are they?**"

"David's very honest with me and sometimes the truth hurts. But I like that - I don't want to be surrounded by 'Yes' people."

"**It's been a great year. I'm getting married and my football club won The Treble.**"

"I can honestly say I don't fancy anyone but David. Honestly."

"**Neither of us are particularly religious. Perhaps we're more spiritual than religious.**"

"If I'd had a more low key wedding, I would have been called a tight cow. As it is, people say we're flash and over the top. Well, that's fine. But *I* know we had the most amazing day."

"When we got to the actual wedding venue, we helped Victoria in with her big dress and David was actually in tears. It was all very moving." VICTORIA'S STYLIST, KENNY HO

"My dress was virginal, but sexy too..."

"My best man, Gary Neville, was nervous... worrying about the speech, the ring, everything."

"I remember the thrones. That was... different." ALAN HANSON

"Sitting on a throne. What's that all about?" ULRIKA JOHNSON

"I feel I should be sitting here with a sceptre in my hand!" VICTORIA

"The truth is the thrones were lovely, but people commented on how uncomfortable I looked sitting on them. I had a bloody tight corset on, a big meringue dress and it was really hot. I was all... rigid."

"I think there was an element of irony to David and Victoria's wedding that went over some people's heads..." ANGUS DEAYTON

"We are trying to buy a house near London. As soon as we do, we'll buy a big table and put the thrones at either end..."
VICTORIA

"The whole thing was tongue in cheek..."
TRUESTEPPER DANE BOWERS

THE BALLAD OF POSH & BECKS ""

"The wedding – in fact, the whole day – was lovely. Very, very romantic." LOUISE ADAMS, VICTORIA'S SISTER

"At the end of the day, there were so many people out there who were poking fun at us, (I thought) if you can't poke fun at yourself, it's pretty sad." VICTORIA

"Our earnings are often exaggerated. When you read in a newspaper: 'Exclusive interview!' they think we've been paid a lorry load of cash. But we really get nothing. Only once, when we sold the rights to our wedding pictures for £1.2 million to *OK!* magazine. We did that to get rid of the paparazzi, and also to have nice wedding pictures. The money was spent on wedding preparations and security. Everything left over, we gave to charity, but I still get flak about how much we earned." VICTORIA

"On a regular month, *OK!* would sell between 500,000 and 600,000 copies. Just the first issue covering David and Victoria's wedding sold nearly 2 *million* copies. In fact, we nearly sold 5 million copies in a month." MARTIN TOWNSEND, FORMER EDITOR, OK!

"On a scale of one to 100, the wedding was a 150!"
JACKIE ADAMS, VICTORIA'S MOTHER

"It was such a fabulous day." DAVID

"The fact is, we wouldn't have done the wedding any differently. Everything went to plan. We could have had lots of celebrities wandering around who didn't really know us, but we did it our way and we don't regret a thing. Our wedding was a fairytale... a dream come true." VICTORIA

"I wasn't actually invited to the wedding. I'm still fairly disappointed about that..." GARY LINEKER

"I kept hearing Victoria saying 'This is my husband.'" DAVID

“I just wanted to say 'I have you. I'm now Victoria Beckham. I'm quite old-fashioned like that.” **VICTORIA**

“I just love the fact I have the same surname as David. I feel much more... famous now. Everyone knows the name Beckham, so it's a wonderful feeling. But I haven't had time to practice my signature yet.”

“The honeymoon was so romantic. I felt so relaxed. In the end, we only had four days. But it was lovely because it was just the three of us. Brooklyn came too. We just couldn't bear to be parted from him.”

“I think David gets more respect (from people than me), because he's considered more talented.”

“David just gets so frustrated sometimes because people think because he doesn't say a lot, he's stupid. But he's actually really smart. Very... deep and spiritual.” **VICTORIA**

THE BALLAD OF POSH & BECKS

Chapter Five

The Little Fella

DAVID AND VICTORIA ON THE BIRTH OF THEIR SON, BROOKLYN IN MARCH, 1999

❝One of David's most attractive qualities is he shares the same family values as me.❞

❝**1998 was a great year and 1999 looks like being even better now that I'm settled in Manchester and have a baby to look forward to...**❞ VICTORIA

❝Victoria never used to be very good with babies. You'd give her one and she looked like she was about to drop it! But then, when I had my own daughter, Liberty, Victoria (changed). She does everything for her – bathes her, feeds her, changes her nappy and treats her as if she's her own baby.❞ **LOUISE ADAMS, VICTORIA'S SISTER**

❝**I am totally ready for fatherhood. The happiest moment of my life was when Victoria told me she was pregnant. In fact, I was so over the moon, I was lost for words. And though the pregnancy wasn't planned, there wasn't a second of doubt in my mind. We both understand what having children involves and we're both ready for the responsibility.**❞

POSH & **BECKS** *Talking*

❝David came in for the first scan and just cried and cried when he saw our baby. Whenever we talk about it, he just smiles... he says: 'You look lovely. You're just keeping our baby warm.' He's so sweet about it.❞

❝**When I was pregnant, I could have pulled out of The Spice Girls tour. But I didn't want to because of the fans. We ended up playing in 100 degrees of heat with me prancing about in a PVC cat-suit, throwing up at the side of the stage in a bloody bucket!**❞

❝Victoria's great. It's nice to have someone in the group in the same position as me. We swap notes. Her legs are skinnier than mine, but her lump's bigger!❞ **A SIMILARLY PREGNANT MEL B**

❝**Oh yeah, Mel B and I waddle around together. The baby is due in two weeks and I'm waddling around all over the place!**❞

❝Towards the end of my pregnancy, I was so huge. I'd sit in a chair positioned in front of the fridge, totally starkers with my massive belly. David used to pull me up from the chair, open the fridge so I could grab some food, then ease me back into the chair. He'd say: 'You look lovely, you know...'❞

❝**A couple of nights before Brooklyn was born, my dad took me to one side and said "You know, when the baby's born and you first set eyes on him, you'll understand how your mother and I feel about you.'**❞ DAVID

❝When I was giving birth, the baby wasn't in a good position. His head wasn't in the right place. So we had to decide really quickly if we were going to do it normally or perform a caesarean. I chose the second option. I didn't want to be stressed, and have the baby suffer as a result... all I was interested in was having a healthy baby.❞

❝**Victoria kept on going on about how hungry she was!**❞

❝I hadn't eaten since the beginning of the afternoon!**❞**

❝I was telling someone later that I loved giving birth, and they said to me 'Are you mad?' But I loved it, absolutely loved it.❞

❝I cried when Brooklyn was born. I wanted to cut his umbilical cord, but the doctor did it so quickly, I didn't get a chance.**❞**
DAVID

❝My mum was at the birth. She videoed it! Not the whole thing obviously, but she videoed me being stitched up. I remember looking up and her saying 'Smile!'❞

❝David was with me in the hospital when I had Brooklyn, and I was completely oblivious to the fact there were thousands of people outside until I turned on the TV and there were *GMTV* broadcasting from Portland Hospital. That completely freaked me out. David was supposed to stay the night in the room next door, but I made him make up a camp bed in my room, so that if anyone tried to get to Brooklyn, they'd have to trample over David's head first!**❞**

THE LITTLE FELLA **❞**

"His name is Brooklyn Joseph, and we are both overjoyed. The birth was natural, and there were no complications, nothing at all. Victoria is very well. She's sitting up drinking champagne and has already spoken to the other Spice Girls."

DAVID MEETS THE PRESS
FOLLOWING THE BIRTH OF HIS SON.

"David and I found out I was pregnant while I was on tour in America. We were actually in Brooklyn, New York.**"**

VICTORIA EXPLAINS
HOW BROOKLYN BECKHAM
GOT HIS NAME

"Brooklyn's beautiful, beautiful." EMMA BUNTON

"We have a new recruit to The Spice Girls club.**"** MEL C

"Our baby boy looks beautiful. He has my nose and David's thighs. We couldn't be happier."

"He has got Victoria's nose, but he's also got my legs, my feet and my toes... *exactly* the same toes as me.**"**

"I don't think we'll name another child after where he or she was conceived... because we did get a certain amount of stick about that. I like Brooklyn as a name, it's quite different, but you couldn't do it all the time. It really depends on where you are. It wouldn't work if you (conceived)... in somewhere like Moscow!" VICTORIA

"As soon as I saw Brooklyn... he became the only thing that really mattered. Him and David. It instantly put my life into perspective. I love him so much it hurts. David feels the same. He's an amazing father."

"Fatherhood is the best thing that's ever happened to me. It's something that can't be beaten."

"Brooklyn's different every day. He eats unbelievably well, so he's gaining weight all the time, and he's started smiling too... especially when he has wind!"

"Brooklyn is awake all through the night every night. That's why I've got these bags under my eyes."

"I quite happy to sit up all night just watching Brooklyn breathe."

"David's much better at changing nappies than me."

"I've always loved kids, so I don't mind getting involved in the mucky side of things." **DAVID**

"I've changed Brooklyn's nappies!" EMMA BUNTON

"If I had my choice, I'd rather Brooklyn was a footballer than a singer." **VICTORIA**

"David's bought a little baby Manchester United football shirt which says 'Beckham' on the back. Ahhhh." VICTORIA

"We always wanted a boy..." **DAVID**

"I'm really excited for David and Victoria. But I hope Brooklyn plays for Liverpool, and not Manchester United!" MEL C

THE LITTLE FELLA

"Brooklyn loves to watch David play, and I like to see Brooklyn enjoying himself." **VICTORIA**

"I'd like Brooklyn to play for Manchester United, of course."

TED BECKHAM, DAVID'S FATHER

"Brooklyn's a really good footballer. He's better than I was at his age. Well, my mum says he is, anyway. Even when he's got a load of toys, he always goes for the football first... it'll be interesting to see how he turns out. I'd love him to go into football." **DAVID**

"I'm going to try and get Brooklyn to study hard at school, even though I know he's going to want to be a footballer!" VICTORIA

"Brooklyn's a handsome little fellow – just like his dad."

SANDRA BECKHAM, DAVID'S MOTHER

"David's not the greatest dancer. He'll kill me for (saying) this, but he can stand at the bar and sway about, and that's about it. Brooklyn was in my tummy in the studio and on tour, so I know he's definitely got rhythm. Imagine him at the school disco – a great footballer with good rhythm – he's going to have great pulling power..."

"If Brooklyn sees David on the telly, he shouts 'Daddy! Daddy!' It must be a little strange for him really..." **VICTORIA**

"When Brooklyn looks through magazines and papers, he must think it's the family photo album!" VICTORIA

"Brooklyn has made me look at life from a whole new perspective. Things that seemed important before just don't seem as important now." **DAVID**

"Brooklyn is the best thing that's ever happened to me. Being a dad is more important than football."

"Many people have said Brooklyn will probably be spoiled. I hope he will. Spoiled with love." **VICTORIA**

"Being a working mother means the balls are always up in the air." VICTORIA

"People sometimes say I should hide Brooklyn away more. But if I do go out, I like to take him with me. He's a normal little boy and I want him to grow up as normal as possible." **VICTORIA**

"It really hurts when the crowds sing 'Is that baby really yours, Beckham?'"

"The most important thing is my son. The thought of him not being safe is too awful to think about. It's something worrying – every parent's worst nightmare." **VICTORIA**

"There's been a lot of stuff in the press about people wanting to kidnap Brooklyn, and I did have threats. But the police were fantastic. Brooklyn has a bodyguard with him now." VICTORIA

THE LITTLE FELLA

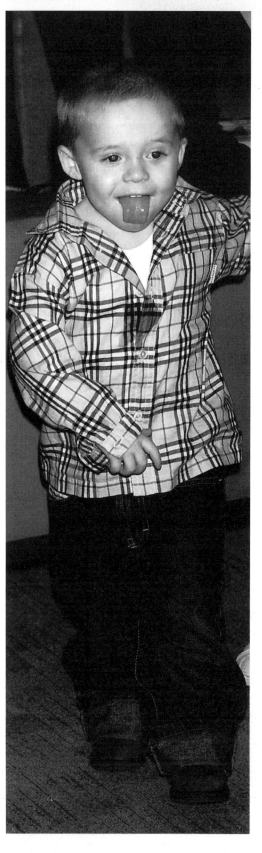

" There have been many stories saying we're selling pictures of Brooklyn, and they're all untrue. I get really angry when I read that stuff because we've never even considered it. We don't want his picture splashed all over the papers. If he wants to do that stuff when he's older, that's his decision. But not now. **"** DAVID

" Brooklyn is not a money-spinner. "

" I'm not the kind of mother who finds it easy to let Brooklyn go off and do his own thing. If he goes out for the day – even if it's with my mum – I'm on the phone every ten minutes. I'm very hands-on. I do find it hard to let him go. My mum says told me when you have a baby, you don't stop worrying from the day you give birth. My mum still worries about *me*. **"**

" As someone with three children of their own, I'll be able to give Victoria a few tips about bringing up Brooklyn. It's never easy with your first, but Brooklyn is beautiful and Victoria is very happy. "
JACKIE ADAMS, VICTORIA'S MOTHER

"It's a challenge to play football against the best players in the world. And it's also a chance to stake a claim for myself."

"The phrase 'Zig-a-zig-ah' means whatever you want it to mean. A kiss, a cuddle... use your imagination!"

"What do I regard as the depth of misery? Spilling red wine on my Armani suit."

"Not many nice shops in Manchester. No Prada, No Gucci..."

"It doesn't get any sweeter than this. It's definitely the most satisfying goal I've scored in my life."

"I love being pregnant. I like giving birth. Actually, I love it!"

"I am so lucky we have such supportive parents. My mum and sister are my best friends." **VICTORIA**

"People can say what they want about me. But David and Brooklyn, they're mine. They can't touch them."

"This is our first child and we've got a lot to learn. But we want to learn together." **VICTORIA**

"Brooklyn has to live like a little boy. He's got to play in the park, do all of those things. The other day, he was saying: 'Mummy, mummy, bus, bus'. I was going to a meeting, so we got on the bus. He plays with other kids. He goes to the cinema. He's a good, fun, little boy."

"I'm quite a relaxed bloke. I'll often let things go over my head rather than let them get to me. Sometimes, it's hard because the attention we get is 'full-on' every day. In fact, not a day goes by without something cropping up in the news about us. Yeah, it's hard, but it makes us a strong family – all three of us."

"Brooklyn loves coming to work with me, and he's really good. He doesn't mind where he is as long as he's with me or David."

"When Brooklyn grows up, we're both unfortunately aware he's never going to get any privacy in his life. It'll probably change from, 'What's happening with David and Victoria?' to 'What's Brooklyn doing?', 'Who's Brooklyn's first girlfriend?' or 'Brooklyn's first car'. But, as parents, we'll try and protect him as much as we can." **DAVID**

"We want to make Brooklyn as anonymous as we can until he's old enough to decide the things he wants to do for himself." VICTORIA

"I do not have a nanny for Brooklyn. I try to be with him as often as I can. One of us will always be with him. If neither of us can make it, our parents help out. We want his childhood to be as normal as possible. His life won't be like... like the Royal Family's." **VICTORIA**

THE LITTLE FELLA

Victoria and David's views on future additions to the Beckham household...

"Motherhood is the best thing to happen to me. But the problem with having a baby is you just want another one! It would be brilliant for Brooklyn to have someone to play with."

"We're going to be like The Waltons and have a house full of children and dogs. I definitely want to have a lot more children now that I've had Brooklyn." VICTORIA

"I think we'd like a couple more children, maybe. But I don't think I'd be able to fit any more names on the tongue of my boot! You see, I usually have the name 'Beckham' on the front of my boot, but now it' 'Brooklyn' with 'Beckham' on the back. I think Adidas are quite pleased actually!"

"I'd love to have a huge, huge family with a big old Christmas tree. That's my ultimate goal. But not right now, because I'm a bit busy!" VICTORIA

"Yeah, that would be nice. I wouldn't have to get to know the in-laws! Brooklyn seems to like blonde girls though. He gets very shy if he sees my friends - even though they're my age – if they have blonde hair. He gets embarrassed and hides his face. He just seems to like them. That could be a problem! (Phoenix) could bleach her hair... she is gorgeous, so you never know."

VICTORIA, ON THE SUBJECT OF BROOKLYN EVENTUALLY
MARRYING MEL B'S DAUGHTER, PHOENIX CHI

"I can't put into words what I feel for Brooklyn. It's a bond between the three of us that started when he was growing in Victoria's womb. It's unbelievable. He's unbelievable. We're a family now."

DAVID

"Brooklyn's a tough little chap. We're all tough in this family. We have to be." VICTORIA

Chapter Six

Leaving The Nest

VICTORIA'S SOLO CAREER, FROM 'OUT OF YOUR MIND' TO HER FIRST SOLO ALBUM...

Victoria's first non-Spice Girls project was the single 'Out Of Your Mind', a collaboration with Dane Bowers and Truesteppers. Pitted against Spiller's 'Groovejet (If This Ain't Love)', featuring Sophie Ellis Bextor on lead vocals, 'Out of Your Mind' reached No.2 in the summer of 2000. Spiller, however, reached No.1...

❝We met in the studio. I was doing the Truesteppers single and Victoria was working with The Spice Girls on their album. I went down to Vic and said, 'Do you want to come and have a listen to this track?' I thought it would be cool to get her involved in the song.**❞ TRUESTEPPER DANE BOWERS**

❝The first thing I did after hearing the track was play it to the girls, because I wanted their opinion. They all said, 'You've got to do this!' It's the first single I've done on my own, so to speak, and the media will say good and bad things about it. But the people that matter are the fans.**❞** VICTORIA

POSH & **BECKS** *Talking*

"For someone who's supposedly only interested in her music, Victoria has been doing a great deal of promotion for this single. I can't think of anything my boyfriend would like less than me dragging him round the shops...**"** SOPHIE ELLIS BEXTOR

"When Victoria was doing all those signings (at Woolworth's), you do tend to think 'Golly, that's quite an eager way to promote your song...'" SOPHIE ELLIS BEXTOR

"I think Dane Bowers is a very strange character...**"**
SOPHIE ELLIS BEXTOR

"It's just... trying to stir up trouble. At the end of the day, 'Groovejet' is a really good song. But the reason I'm angry is because (by going up against me in the charts), I think, 'Is this their way of getting themselves in the papers?' I mean, how else is Spiller going to get in the papers?" VICTORIA

"My daughter is the real Posh Spice!**"**
JANET ELLIS, FORMER BLUE PETER PRESENTER AND MOTHER OF SOPHIE ELLIS BEXTOR

"(When I saw her), Victoria didn't say anything to me. I suppose they're was nothing to say." SOPHIE ELLIS BEXTOR, 2000

"The Spiller song was a great song. I've met Sophie now and she's a nice girl.**"** VICTORIA, 2001

"I've met Victoria now. She's quite nice. She was only two dressing rooms away from me at a TV show, so I went and said, 'Hello'. I thought it was time to lay the whole rivalry thing to rest. We were both very polite, and she was very nice to me. We get on fine, so that's that." SOPHIE ELLIS BEXTOR, 2001

"Personally, I think it's a great shame people looked at my record as if it had failed, just because it got to Number Two. To me, it was a great success. It showed me there were people out there willing to buy a record by me, rather than me as part of The Spice Girls.**"** VICTORIA

Victoria's first solo single, 'Not Such An Innocent Girl', found itself doing battle with Kylie Minogue's 'Can't Get you Out Of My Head' in September, 2001. As with 'Out Of Your Mind' a year before, Victoria had to be content with No. 2.

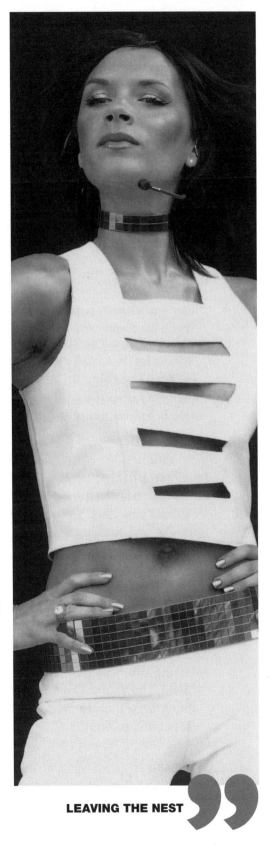

❝'Not Such An Innocent Girl' is me saying 'Don't judge a book by its' cover. Look a bit deeper.'❞ VICTORIA

❝I rang my manager as soon as I heard (the single release dates clashed), and asked whether we could change the date, but it would have been a nightmare. Also, I'd only have been up against someone else. Then I sent a note because it was getting crazy and I felt it was just human courtesy. I just said, 'Supposedly we're at war, but it's not like that'. There's no ill feeling. The cards have been dealt and I just thought I should play the game and go along with it. She's a tough cookie. I imagine she can handle herself.❞ KYLIE MINOGUE

❝It's hard to compete with someone who has three decades worth of fans.❞
VICTORIA ON KYLIE'S LONG-ESTABLISHED APPEAL

LEAVING THE NEST 🙼

KYLIE MINOGUE

"It's fine for Victoria to say I've had hits in three different decades, but I wasn't in The Spice Girls. It always depends on the song. People either like it or they don't." **KYLIE MINOGUE**

"I'm not disappointed. I said from the beginning I'd be happy with 'Top Ten'. Kylie's done really well, but obviously she's been doing this a lot longer than I have." VICTORIA

"I like the Kylie record – I've always liked Kylie, she's great at what she does. In fact, I've got nothing bad to say about her at all..."

VICTORIA

In September 2001, Victoria released her first solo album...

"Acting is something I definitely want to do... you know, films. But first, I'm going to write an album myself. A solo album..."

"To be honest, I really haven't got a clue who my fans really are. So, as a solo artist, I have work to establish myself. And, of course, I don't expect to be huge at the beginning of my solo career."

"People say, 'You don't have to do this solo stuff. You've got David, you've got The Spice Girls'. And I know, in a way, I'm lining myself up to be pulled down. It's like dodging bullets! But I need to do this."

"The reason why I was the last Spice Girl to put out any solo stuff is that I just didn't have the guts to do it. I was very nervous because

I knew I was going to be really criticised no matter what I did. Because there was a vocoder on 'Out Of Your Mind', people were saying 'Oh, Posh can't sing!' I knew there was going to be pressure…"

"It does hit hard if you're being told every day you can't sing or you can't dance. And that's exactly what I was being told by the media on a daily basis. I'd had enough of it really. Then David began to build up my confidence."

"David was the backbone behind my album. He gave me the confidence to do it. When people say 'Can she sing?' or 'Can she do this or that?' I'm not going to lie, that knocks your confidence. But it was David who built up my confidence and said 'Get in there and do it. You want to do it. You love doing it.'"

"She wasn't confident about doing a solo album and needed a little push. So I gave her a little push." DAVID

LEAVING THE NEST

"In the past, I was one of The Spice Girls. They were very loud, very bubbly and I was in the background, really. But with my book, my album and my website, I'm coming out more. Also, I'm a lot more light-hearted than people might think. My tongue is very often firmly lodged in my cheek."

"My autobiography is straight from the horse's mouth. Not that I'm saying I'm a horse..." VICTORIA

"Prince Charles asked me if David and I had any plans to do a duet. I said 'No way!'" **VICTORIA**

"I'm no opera singer. I've never claimed to be. And I'm not saying I'm the next Whitney Houston either..." VICTORIA

"People do find it difficult to take me seriously as a solo artist, and of course, I do understand that. They want me to prove I can do it – to write songs, to sing live. They know Posh Spice, they know Posh and Becks, but they don't know Victoria Beckham."

"Yes, I can wear high heels and shop on Bond Street and look like I'm a miserable cow, but at the same time I am a singer and a songwriter and that's what I do. Let the media say what they want – it's the fans who will hopefully buy my records."

"80% of artists mime at things like *Party At The Park*. However, I can assure you – I *can* sing and I *can* dance."

"Everything on my album is the best that I could do. I was lucky enough to work with some fantastic writers and producers... real A-list people. I think it's a fantastic pop album."

"'Not Such An Innocent Girl' is totally different from my first single (with Dane Bowers) and The Truesteppers. That was R&B, but this is mainly pop. The writers I worked with on the album knew this, that I wanted what I know best – pop music."

"There are two big ballads that I wrote for David on the LP – 'Unconditional Love' and 'IOU'. 'Unconditional Love' is a ballad all about our relationship, and 'IOU' explains that I wouldn't be where I am today without him. Like the song says 'I owe him everything... I'd be nothing without him'. I have really opened my heart."

"I play her album in my car." **DAVID**

"It's brilliant. Two years of my life have gone into reaching this peak – the single, the album, my website, my book. Everything is finally ready." VICTORIA

"I live off stress. I love it. It's like an adrenaline thing. I've got so much respect for women out there who are working mums. Even when we were recording, I had a crèche for Brooklyn in the studio."

"There's also a song on my new album called 'Every Part Of Me'. It's about Brooklyn, and he actually sings on it. When he hears it, he goes 'Brooklyyyyn!'"

"Brooklyn likes my album, because it's got good strong beats and it's good to dance to. He recognises my voice and says 'Mummy singing' and 'Brooklyn song'. But then he gets all shy. When people come round, he whispers 'Mummy, Brooklyn's song'. He likes me to play it to people. **"**

"I don't have a big voice and I'm definitely not the best dancer in the world, but I work hard and at the same time keep house and bring up my child. People know how hard that is. Up until now, they called me 'Posh', and imagined I'm some bimbo with a pretty face, expensive clothes and high heels. Few of them realised 'Posh' works her butt off, cooks dinner and also finds the time to take her child for a stroll. **"**

"There is a lot of pressure on me. There's always pressure from a record company. You always want to please your boss, but that's the same in any job. The pressure (exists) because people are obviously saying 'Posh Spice, what is she going to do?' But, I've put two years of my life into this, so I really hope people like it. **"**

"If the right acting role came up, I'd probably have a go at it. But music is my priority. I want to stay doing music for as long as I can. **"**

"When the fans say 'I find you inspiring, I love what you do' or 'You put a smile on my face', it makes you think 'This is the reason I'm doing this'. I just put the rest of the rubbish behind me. After all, I've got great songs, a great band and the fans seem to love it. **"**

"I'm really proud when I look back on The Spice Girls. It's only now I appreciate everything we achieved. We were always so busy. I think of what I'd give to have a fraction of that success as a solo artist. **"**

"I really hope people like the album because it would be nice to be in the papers for the right reasons – my music – rather than where I've gone to dinner. **"**

"I was always known as Posh the starlet, wife of the England captain. Now, people can see and hear what I'm really like: deep and real. **"**

LEAVING THE NEST

Chapter Seven

Swings&Roundabouts

DAVID BECKHAM'S TWO MOST IMPORTANT GAMES: HIS SENDING OFF AGAINST ARGENTINA IN WORLD CUP '98, AND ENGLAND'S BATTLE WITH GREECE TO QUALIFY FOR WORLD CUP 2002...

Beckham's lowliest footballing moment surely came in World Cup '98. In a critical qualifying match against old adversaries, Argentina, he was sent off following a foul on Diego Simeone. Reduced to ten men, England subsequently lost the game, and exited the competition. What follows is a record of the incident and the effect it had on David's life...

"I never looked forward to anything in my professional life as much as I did to World Cup '98. Like all football-mad kids, I grew up watching the greatest players on television battling it out for the biggest team prize in sport. What happened was... unfortunate."

"It was like the Kennedy thing – 'Where were you the night the president was shot?' In Elizabethan times, Becks would have been sent to the Tower and had his feet chopped off!"

RICHARD E. GRANT

POSH & **BECKS** *Talking*

"I was sitting on the England bench at the time. I saw David kick out at the Argentine and thought 'He's off'.**"**

PAUL MERSON

"I was shouting 'What are you doing? What are you doing?!'"

SUPERMODEL JODIE KIDD

"I couldn't believe the ref sent him off for such an innocent little kick.**"** **GARY LINEKER**

GARY LINEKER

"Let's just say the referee fell into a trap. It was a difficult decision to avoid because I went down well, and in moments like that, there's always tension. You could say my falling down transformed a yellow card into a red card. But in fact, the most appropriate punishment was a yellow card. Obviously, I was being clever. By letting myself fall, I got the referee to pull out a red card immediately. In reality, David's (kick) wasn't a violent blow. It was just a little kick with no force behind it... probably just instinctive. But the referee was right there and punished his intention to retaliate."

ARGENTINE INTERNATIONAL DIEGO SIMEONE, THE PLAYER DAVID 'KICKED'

"The sending off was pretty straightforward. The rules are very clear about kicking or attempting to kick an opponent. In that type of situation, one person has to be punished. If I hadn't has sent him off, I would have been punished for not following the rules. But I was quite surprised by the reaction after the game...**"**

REFEREE KIM MILTON NEILSON

"That ref nearly ruined David's life. I actually don't know how Beckham coped with it. When you read the papers in the next few days, he'd been getting bullets in the post. I think I'd have moved to Outer Mongolia." PAUL MERSON

“Ten heroic lions, one stupid boy.” **DAIRY MIRROR HEADLINE**

“It's generally safer to have nothing to do with journalists. They put unnecessary pressure on players, managers – even referees – and I find it hard to understand how people who claim to love the game of football try so hard to damage it.” DAVID

“There's no need to look for scapegoats. David didn't do it on purpose, it's a mistake he made, and he will learn from that mistake. He's very upset about the whole thing, (because) he's realised the gravity of what he's done. He's still a young lad, and of course, all this criticism... is something that is going to be very hard for him to deal with.”
FORMER ENGLAND MANAGER GLENN HODDLE

“Of course I re-lived that moment. Two days before the Argentina game I was a hero. Then the next day, they wanted me hung. People can be so fickle.”

“We will see an even better David Beckham because of this.”
MANCHESTER UNITED/ENGLAND TEAM MATE PHIL NEVILLE

GLENN HODDLE

“Because I went straight to America after World Cup '98, my family bore the brunt of what was coming to me. That was a big thing for them, because they're not used to that sort of stuff. For normal people, handling 20 or 30 journalists outside your door is definitely not something you're used to, and my mum, dad and the rest of my family did amazingly well.”

“The abuse that boy got...” **ACTOR JAMES 'COLD FEET' NESBITT**

SWINGS & ROUNDABOUTS

"I suppose booing was (the fans') way of getting back at me."

"Actually, I feel safest *on* the field. Even though I can hear what people are saying or chanting, I can concentrate... enjoy the game. I can keep them quiet by scoring a goal."

"David does take a severe amount of people slagging him off. Do they do that to Ronaldo in Italy? I don't think so. They put him up on a pedestal and said 'Good bloke. You're a talented player who works hard'. Then if he went to (another country), it'd be 'Oh, why is he going?' Well, why do you think?" VICTORIA

"At one point, I couldn't see any light at the end of the tunnel. There was nothing I could say or do to make it stop..."

"Obviously, it's going to be difficult when people are using your head as a dartboard..." VICTORIA

"What David had to go through was nothing short of scandalous. I couldn't understand it. People can say what they want about you off the pitch, but he answered everybody's with his performances *on* the pitch." **GARY NEVILLE**

"The shouts certainly didn't affect his football, because he was fantastic every time he put on a shirt for Manchester united or England." MICHAEL OWEN

"I just sat it out. That's always been my mentality. I'd had previous knocks in my career and I just wanted the opportunity to show people I could do my best – both for my club and my country."

"The past year must have been so hard to take for David. It's been a joke, and a sick one at that, the way he's been jeered every tie he got the ball. Yet, he's handled it brilliantly and is playing better than ever. I'd like to think we've all helped him. There are no superstars in our dressing room,

so we all give him plenty of stick. That's the way it works with us – you take the mickey out of each other. A good laugh not only eases the strain but brings you all closer together. **"**

MANCHESTER UNITED TEAM MATE
RYAN GIGGS

"The Manchester United players and fans never doubted me, and that's the reason I'm still here and playing well. **"**

"If I do get into scrapes sometimes, I put it down to a certain side of my game. But it's not one I want to lose, because it's part of me. I just want to win everything all the time. That's why some of these things happen. I don't do it maliciously. It's just my will to win. **"**

"David has a wonderful skill and a wonderful attitude to the game. He wants to be a great footballer. Unfortunately, he sometimes falls foul of officialdom... and that's what happened here. Sadly, the consequences were enormous. **"**

FORMER ENGLAND MANAGER
GLENN HODDLE

"(In the end), the sending off made grow up, realise a few things about myself... **"**

DAVID WITH HIS BEST PAL
AND ENGLAND TEAM-MATE
GARY NEVILLE

SWINGS & **ROUNDABOUTS** **"**

"There is no way I would have survived the World Cup incident without Victoria. She didn't say anything, just gave me this big cuddle. She was about a month pregnant — and no-one knew but us. In the end, I think she was as pleased to see me as I was her. Once I was with her, I *knew* I'd get through it."

"Let's not forget, he's a fantastic footballer... which is the be all and end all." ALAN SHEARER

"England had a mountain of courage and a molehill of luck in that game. Unfortunately, of course, certain things happened that... shouldn't have happened." **PRIME MINISTER TONY BLAIR**

"I have seen the game many times on video since, and I would not change any of my decisions." REFEREE KIM MILTON NIELSEN

"When I'm feeling down about myself, thinking 'Why do people think that about me?' or 'Why are they saying that?' what better person can I look to than my own husband to see how someone can turn everything around?" **VICTORIA**

"What happened against Argentina does not still haunt me. I think a lot of people would like to think it still does. But you move on from these things. You have to, otherwise they can affect you. I've moved on now and I'm a stronger person for it."

"According to the Argentine players, Beckham's kick was the worst they had ever seen. According to the English players, it was nothing. There's war in the world... people dying everywhere. Yet, in England, the biggest problem is one player who made a small mistake in a football match. I think that's bad."

KIM MILTON NIELSON

"There are more important things in life than football." DAVID

SWINGS & ROUNDABOUTS

The World Cup Qualifier

On October 8th, 2002, England played Greece at Old Trafford. If they won or drew the game, the team would automatically qualify for the World Cup finals in 2002. David Beckham's contribution to the match assured him a place in footballing history...

❝This is the game, that if we win, means we're through to the World Cup. That means a massive amount to the players. We also know it means a lot to the entire nation. But we've not worked so hard in the last few months to lose this game. It's in our hands, so we can make it or break it.❞ **DAVID**

❝**We are the favourites. If we go out, play well against Greece and have the right attitude, getting a result won't be a problem. Hopefully.**❞ ENGLAND'S STEVEN GERRARD

❝We are not so bad, you know...❞ **GREECE'S NIKOS DABIZAS**

SVEN GORAN ERIKSSON

❝**It's 1-nil to Greece!**❞

MATCH OF THE DAY'S JOHN MOTSON

❝We didn't play that well, especially in the first half. Greece deserved 1-0 at half time.❞

**ENGLAND MANAGER
SVEN GORAN ERIKSSON**

❝**Sherringham has equalised for England!**❞

SKY SPORTS' MARTIN TYLER

❝One minute later, and Greece have gone ahead again...❞

JOHN MOTSON

" Greece continued to play well. We struggled. Maybe we wanted it just too much. **"** SVEN GORAN ERIKKSON

" We couldn't get our tempo going. The crowd got upset. We got upset. It made us panicky. We just had to dig deep, and I think the captain showed us how. David ran his feet into the ground, gave a tremendous performance. He deserved everything. **"** ENGLAND GOAL-SCORER TEDDY SHERINGHAM

" Teddy's a nice bloke... and a great player. We're both cockneys so we understand each other! **"** DAVID

" David Beckham raised that England team by its' bootlaces in the last fifteen minutes... **"** MATCH OF THE DAY'S MARK LAWRENCESON

" Beckham lines up for the free kick. Is this one of those moments? **"** MARTIN TYLER

DAVID WITH TEDDY SHERINGHAM
AND GIRLFRIEND NIKKI SMITH

SWINGS & **ROUNDABOUTS**

"Great players rise to great occasions..."

HENRY WINTER, *THE DAILY TELEGRAPH*

"As Becks put that ball down... I shouted to him, This is our last chance. He knew he had only 20 seconds to save us. He knew that if he didn't score, we were going through to the play-offs. But if anybody can cope with that kind of pressure, it's Becks."

ENGLAND DEFENDER GARY NEVILLE

"I just couldn't bear the tension..." JOANNE BECKHAM, DAVID'S SISTER

"Luckily, we have the best player in the world at taking free kicks..." SVEN GORAN ERIKKSON

"I knew this was my last throw of the dice..." DAVID

"When he went up to take that free kick, I was willing him to score. I can't tell you how I felt when the ball went in. It was just fantastic... I was so proud of him." VICTORIA

"Yes, yes for England! David Beckham has done it!" MARTIN TYLER

"To be honest, one had to go in. I'd had quite a few free kicks and was disappointed with most of them. But then, I got my chance. Teddy said to me 'I'll have it'. But I thought 'It's a bit too far out for him'. Somehow, I just fancied it... I had a good feeling."

DAVID

"As soon as David scored, we knew we just had to wait it out for the final whistle..." ENGLAND DEFENDER MARTIN KEOWN

"When the game finally ended, every player on that pitch congratulated Beckham. A great goal. A tremendous player. An absolute hero."

FORMER ENGLAND STRIKER TREVOR BROOKING

"When you think about what he went through after being sent off against Argentina in World Cup '98, it was a phenomenal turnaround. As far as his England team-mates were concerned, he was certainly a king."

ENGLAND GOALKEEPER, NIGEL MARTYN

"As a captain, David rose to the challenge. You could see the respect his team-mates have for him. He embodies everything good about English football."

FOOTBALL ASSOCIATION CHIEF, ALAN CROZIER

"With David Beckham, everybody talks about the skill, but for me, it's the work. When England were struggling and needed a hero, he stood up and was counted. He is a role model on and off the field and a true captain." **HENRY WINTER,** *THE DAILY TELEGRAPH*

"In terms of drama, I have never witnessed anything like that match. We owe everything to David."

FORMER ENGLAND STRIKER, TREVOR FRANCIS

"David played one of the best games I have ever seen him play. He was a real captain for his country, and I'm *so* glad he scored that goal." **SVEN GORAN ERIKKSON**

"We didn't play the prettiest of games. They kept coming back and we just had to keep battling. But, as I've said before, the character of the players is unbelievable. For a young team to go 1-nil under, then equalise, go 2-1 down and then come back again... it just showed how much we wanted it." DAVID

"For England, it was a poor performance. But, in the way that great players do, David Beckham did everything. He worked harder than everyone... played better than everyone. At one point, he was taking on great clumps of Greek defenders on his own. It was quite extraordinary." **PAUL HAYWARD,** *THE DAILY TELEGRAPH*

SWINGS & ROUNDABOUTS

❝Greece made it a very difficult game for us. They're an extremely capable side. Yes, it was tough game, but we showed the necessary resolve to come through it.❞

ENGLAND DEFENDER RIO FERDINAND

❝Now that the party's over, we have to be honest. It was a very poor England performance. Being fair to Greece, both of England's goals came from free kicks given for non-existent fouls. Cheating, basically. But that said, I still feel England has a very good chance of wining the next World Cup.❞

PATRICK BARCLAY, *THE SUNDAY TELEGRAPH*

❝The referee gave a festival of free kicks for David Beckham. Both England goals came from free kicks when there had been no foul. England is a country of the gentleman, but I must say the referee was not acceptable.❞ GREEK COACH, OTTO REHAGEL

❝David Beckham virtually played Greece on his own.❞ **JOHN MOTSON**

❝We were mentally fit and capable of very good things. We showed it today.❞

NIKOS DABIZAS

❝It was David that won that match. He played like a true captain, and showed he really is the best player in the world. Right now, I love him.❞
COMEDIAN FRANK SKINNER

❝It looked like we were heading out of the competition, but we did it... thanks to David Beckham.❞
CHAT SHOW HOST MICHAEL PARKINSON

FRANK SKINNER

"David Beckham should be knighted. It was a great result and I'm still crying." **SIR RICHARD BRANSON**

"Beckham's performance was unique. Never before have I ever seen a player carry an entire team on his back at international level. Not Johan Cruyff, not Pele, not Maradona, not Zidane. He swept England up in his arms and carried them to the World Cup finals despite themselves. One day... the Queen will bestow the nation's highest honour upon one extremely proud subject: David Beckham. There is only one question... Why wait, Ma'am?"

JOHN SADLER, *THE SUN*

"I'm very proud to be Mrs. Beckham today..." **VICTORIA**

"The game was the first step to something that could be very beautiful. Let's be happy today. Tomorrow, let's try to be better."

SVEN GORAN ERIKKSON

"I just couldn't have written a script like that. Captaining my country and scoring the goal at Old Trafford that took us through to the World Cup finals. That's fairytale stuff, isn't it?"

"Captain Golden Balls!"
THE SUNDAY PEOPLE

"I've certainly lived up to my wife's nickname for me. I'm sure Victoria will be calling me 'Golden Balls'... tonight!"

SWINGS & ROUNDABOUTS

Chapter Eight

Has One Seen The Football Pitch?

VICTORIA AND DAVID AIR THEIR VIEWS ON LIFE AT 'BECKINGHAM PALACE', HOME COOKING AND THE PRICE OF FAME...

"My dream was a big house with a moat, dragons and a fort to keep people out!"

"(Our) house is beautiful. It's quite modern, and we designed the rooms ourselves so it's all really personal to us."

"It's such a beautiful home. It took two years to finish and we're both so in love with it. The house has six bedrooms, and every room is themed. Our bedroom is very calm, with lots of white, and Brooklyn's room is amazing! I said to David, 'Can you believe it? We're 26 and 27 and we don't have a mortgage.' It's a big achievement."

"We've had a football pitch built at home for David and Brooklyn. It's actually a proper pitch, with underground watering. And do you know what they do? Put mummy in goal. Can you imagine? One gust of wind and I'm over!"

POSH & **BECKS** *Talking*

"I've got white carpets and Brooklyn has been sick all over them. He rides his scooter into my curtains too. I'm used to sick and poo!"

"The best thing about the house is it's private. No one can see it and no one's going to see it..."

"When I get home, I shut the door and think 'Wow! This is what I worked so hard for.'"

"People think I wander around the house in heels and a designer dress. But I do have towelling dressing gowns and dodgy tracksuits. And I put a hat on to solve bad hair days when I'm out."

"We go shopping, get the food we really like and some Asti Spumante or Tesco's Bucks Fizz. Then we cuddle up and watch *Friends*."

"I can sit there for hours and not say anything to David while being blissfully happy just watching television."

"For the first time in my life, I'm happy. I'm not Posh Spice to David and he's not a famous soccer star to me. We'd rather be cuddled up on the sofa watching *Blind Date* with a takeaway curry than out at a club."

"I'm not very domesticated. I can't really cook, so I do these ready-made meals that you just pierce at the top and stick in the oven for a couple of minutes. David, on the other hand, does everything. He cooks, he cleans, he's brilliant."

"David got that obsessive-compulsive thing where's everything's got to match. If you open our fridge, it's all co-ordinated. If there's only three cans of Diet Coke, he'll throw one away rather than have three – that's uneven."

"It's nice to go out to these parties occasionally. We'll sit down for 30 minutes or so, then go home, put on our pyjamas and get an Indian takeaway."

"David and I have these really loud checked pyjamas. I wear them and those big slippers with dogs on. The slippers are great, but if you don't walk right in them, you could trip downstairs and break your neck!**"**

"I'd rather live in a council flat with David than in 'Beckingham Palace' without him."

The price of fame...

"Having fun and also being successful is a bonus.**"**
VICTORIA

"I'm not flash. I do like having nice things and a good lifestyle... not because of the image they portray to the outside world, but because they make me happy." VICTORIA

"Money matters. It gives you security for the present and the future. When I want a rest, or to go on holiday, I can't just stop at any hotel. You have to travel far to get away from everything. Rent a house. Hire security. It all costs money. I've realised that when you're famous, you have to buy your freedom.**" VICTORIA**

"My first car cost £80,000. But my Dad didn't really like it. He's thinks it's nice, but not the sort of thing he'd go for. He'd get a big, comfortable... exactly!" DAVID

HAS ANY ONE SEEN THE FOOTBALL PITCH?

"I can tell you exactly what I spend on food and petrol... and how much my car insurance costs. I do look at the price of things because I don't have the kind of money everyone thinks I do. I'm not going to pretend I'm skint, but I don't have £28 million! In fact, David never looks at the price of anything. It's the one thing he and I differ on. But I'm not going to be a nag bag. I'm here to make him happy." VICTORIA

"People read in the papers about how much money I'm supposed to earn, where I live... where I go on holiday. They probably think 'Flash git'. But that's not how I see myself." DAVID

"David and I do a lot of stuff for charity. We're forever signing things, like football shirts and costumes, and auctioning them off. But we try to keep that side of our lives private." VICTORIA

"The dogs eat better than David and I do. They have dinner from Marks & Spencer every night... They wolf down about ten chickens. It's like feeding horses!" VICTORIA

"I don't really socialise a lot. If you add up the number of times David and I have been to premieres or launch parties, you could probably count it on one hand. We go out on Saturday night and we see our families. I've got a couple of really good friends but people do surprise you when they go to the newspapers and let you down – friends, people you've employed, ex-boyfriends... I do find it hard to trust people now."

Chapter Thirteen

My Left Foot...

ON 10 APRIL 2002, DAVID BECKHAM BROKE THE SECOND METATARSAL BONE IN HIS LEFT FOOT WHILE PLAYING FOR MANCHESTER UNITED IN A 3-2 WIN OVER DEPORTIVO LA CORUNA IN THE CHAMPION'S LEAGUE.

The injury cast immediate doubt over Beckham's chances of leading England into the World Cup:

"When I stood up, I knew I'd broken something. The first question I asked the surgeon was if I was out of the World Cup. I was devastated." **DAVID**

"David called me from the hospital to let me know how he was. To be honest, he was devastated. He's very, very upset, in plaster and in a lot of pain. He said he was more upset because of the games coming up. I feel sorry for him. It's a terrible thing to have happened, but fingers crossed, he'll be OK..."
TED BECKHAM, DAVID'S FATHER

"This is a real blow for David personally, for Manchester United and for England, but there is nothing we can do about it. I am sure, however, that the medical staff at Manchester United will do everything in their power to ensure David recovers fully and quickly." **SVEN-GORAN ERIKSSON**

POSH & **BECKS** *Talking*

"Managers can name a replacement for an injured player up to 24 hours before the tournament starts. Therefore, Sven-Goran Eriksson has until 30 May to decide whether to include David Beckham in his final 23-man England squad." FIFA REPRESENTATIVE

"The prognosis is slightly better. Clearly, with an injury of this type, the first 48 hours are crucial, but things do sound a little better. Hopefully, David's foot will improve." FA CHIEF EXECUTIVE ALAN CROZIER

"David is young. He'll play in other matches." SIR ALEX FERGUSON

"Let's not forget, David's unbelievably fit. And he's a quick healer." MANCHESTER UNITED COACH, ERIC HARRISON

"I didn't like the oxygen tent. I tried it out, but I just couldn't sleep in it. They say you have to spend eight hours in it – I couldn't spend eight minutes in it! I hate the thing. It might work for some people, but not for me." DAVID NIXES THE OXYGEN TANK CURE

"I'm not a miracle worker, but if millions of people focus their mind on David's foot, we can unleash a powerful healing force. I want people to touch their TV screens. Take it seriously – if just for a few seconds – send David some healing energy." URI GELLER SENDS HEALTH RAYS TO DAVID'S FOOT VIA GMTV

"The Prime Minister has pointed out that nothing is more important to England's arrangements for the World Cup than the state of David Beckham's left foot." SPOKESMAN FOR PRIME MINISTER, TONY BLAIR

"I've had lots of offers of treatment from all over the world. I've also had lots of letters of support and really have to thank my fans. Also, the people at Manchester United have been great with me – every minute of the day, using things like laser treatment." DAVID

"With Ronaldo and Zidane, David Beckham is one of the biggest superstars in the world. If he doesn't come to Japan and South Korea, it will hurt the World Cup."
YOSHIHIKO KONNO
SPORTS EDITOR, *DAILY SPORT*

"It's difficult when David wants to be out there playing and he can't. It's just very frustrating for him.... hobbling around the house. But it's not easy for me either. Obviously Brooklyn needs a lot of attention, and with me being heavily pregnant, it's hard for me to pick him up – Brooklyn's really heavy. But we're coping. It's just nice to have David home.**"** **VICTORIA**

"Victoria's been unbelievable. Six months pregnant and she's getting me cups of tea. I've been on crutches for three weeks and she's been carrying everything, including Brooklyn. It's been hard work for her, but she's been amazing." DAVID

"My foot's still a bit sore, but I'm going to get fit. It shouldn't be much of a problem. After all, there are still three weeks left to the start of the World Cup...**"** **DAVID**

"Don't worry, David will be fit. He's done all the training. I think he has sufficient time – there's no big rush. He's a naturally fit athlete and it's not a big mountain for him to climb. It's within David's capacity to lift himself. After all, he's a player who enjoys the big stage – he thrives on it." SIR ALEX FERGUSON

"David is ready. England are ready. Let's see...**"** **SVEN-GORAN ERIKSSON**

MY LEFT FOOT...

Chapter Fourteen

We Can Do This...

❝I want to be the new Bobby Moore. I know I'm following in the footsteps of England captains like him. Bobby Moore walked into a room and people stood up and clapped. He was a gentleman and a great captain. That's always stuck in my mind.**❞**

DAVID ON LEADING ENGLAND INTO THE 2002 WORLD CUP FINALS

❝David will be able to compete in our first World Cup game against Sweden. We've assessed him – free kicks, shooting and lots and lots of running. Until last week, we didn't know who to play on the right. We had options, but not another Beckham. But I'm now confident he'll be able to withstand tackles. I'm very, very optimistic.❞ SVEN-GORAN ERIKSSON

❝I want to make an impression at this World Cup. I've worked harder over the last seven weeks than I ever have to be fit. All the players are ready and I'm confident we can do well.**❞** **DAVID**

❝I have a feeling my time has come.❞

DAVID'S REACTION TO TRYING ON HIS NEW ADIDAS 'NINJA' FOOTBALL BOOTS.

❝My left foot feels a lot better, thanks. When you break a bone, you don't know what's going to happen, but I always had it in my mind I'd be fit for the Swedish game. I'm confident I can last the full 90 minutes. It wouldn't be fair to the rest of the squad if I wasn't sure.**❞** **DAVID**

POSH & **BECKS** *Talking*

66 It's amazing when 20 people chase our coach chanting 'David' or 'Michael'. But our focus has to remain on the players, the staff and the Sweden game. We honestly believe we can beat them and go on from there. 99 DAVID

66 There's no point going into the World Cup thinking you're going to draw or get beaten. We want to go as far as we can. We're not out here for a laugh or a joke. This is the 'Group of Death' and we're in it. 99 DAVID

Sunday, 3 June 2002
England 1 Sweden 1

66 Same Old Story For Sven's Men 99 *DAILY EXPRESS* HEADLINE

66 If we play like that again, we'll definitely be in trouble. We just can't afford to sit back. For me, after two months out, and in the humidity, I was a bit tired. To be honest, my legs disappeared in the second half. That's never happened to me before. 99 DAVID

66 We're disappointed we didn't beat Sweden, but I'm pleased we're going to face Argentina. I'm very proud to be leading my country out against them. For us, it doesn't get much bigger than Argentina – unless it's the World Cup Final itself. 99 DAVID

66 England's results against Argentina in the past have not been good, but that's in the past. 99 DAVID

66 I know a little bit of the story between England and Argentina. But if you go into the match in a sporting way, with a great desire to win, that's a positive thing. But if you look or revenge and feel only hate, that's very dangerous... This is the game to find out about the young players. Hopefully, David can last the full 90 minutes. Of course, he is our captain and we expect a lot of him in such a big game. But we'll just have to wait and see... 99

SVEN-GORAN ERIKSSON

Friday, June 7 2002

England 1 Argentina 0

"Up Yours Senors!" **FRONT PAGE HEADLINE, THE SUN**

"**Foot Of God – Becks Ends Four Years Of Hurt**"

BACK PAGE HEADLINE, *THE SUN*

"It doesn't get any sweeter than this. It's definitely the most satisfying goal I've scored in my life." **DAVID ON HIS MATCH-WINNING PENALTY**

"**I just wanted to put the ghost to rest after my World Cup got turned upside down four years ago. I don't usually get nervous taking penalties but this time I was. I just ran up and hit it as hard as I could. I caught it cleanly and was just so happy it went in.**" DAVID

"Actually, Sir Alex rang me the night before the game and said 'Good luck, enjoy it and pace yourself'. And I did." **DAVID**

WE CAN DO THIS...

"The team showed such courage, such bravery. I might have scored the penalty, but from David Seaman in goal all the way up to the front two, the whole side was magnificent." DAVID

"Nigeria look strong and have players capable of hurting us. Of course, we're still on a high after the Argentina match, but we have to get our attitude right. To slip up now would be ridiculous..." DAVID

England 0 Nigeria 0

"The temperature was right up there – and the humidity. But we played a better game. We slowed it down." SOL CAMPBELL

Saturday, 16 June 2002
England 3 Denmark 0

"Goldane Balls!" FRONT PAGE HEADLINE, *SUNDAY PEOPLE*

"England played well, but I'm especially proud of David. We spoke before the game and he said he felt really fit and up for it. He didn't score today, but he was still a brilliant captain. It's just a shame (because of the pregnancy) I can't be there to see it in person." VICTORIA

"It's a shame Victoria couldn't come. But she's seven and a half months pregnant and it might be dangerous for her. Anyway, she doesn't mind me kissing the goal-scorers. As long as they're boys, she won't be bothered!" DAVID

"I'm so proud of the team. They're not afraid to play real football. They're all heroes." DAVID

"We don't care who we come up against... now, bring on Brazil!"
DAVID

Friday, 21 June 2002

England 1 Brazil 2

❝Anyone For Tennis?**❞** FRONT PAGE HEADLINE, THE MIRROR

❝You worked hard out there. You did a good job. It's not your fault he fluked it, is it? Eh? Eh?❞

DAVID BECKHAM CONSOLES GOALKEEPER DAVID SEAMAN AFTER RONALDINHO'S
FREAK GOAL SENT ENGLAND OUT OF THE WORLD CUP FINALS

❝I just want to say sorry to the rest of the lads and the people back home. It was a fluke goal. Sometimes, that's just the way it goes.**❞**

DAVID (BECKHAM)

❝We could have won this tournament. We were close, but not close enough. I hoped we could do a little better. It's a pity, but I have no regrets... I'm staying put, and so is my team. We'll be back for World Cup 2006 – wiser and stronger. I'm just proud to be the England manager.❞ SVEN-GORAN ERIKSSON

❝To reach the Quarter Finals with a team full of players in their first World Cup is some achievement. We should be proud of ourselves for reaching this point. I had a funny feeling we were going to go all the way, but it wasn't meant to be. But we have to thank our fans for sticking with us and Japan and South Korea – the way they supported us was amazing. I'd rather be staying on than going home, but it's been a fantastic experience for us all. I think the England team will come back all the better for what we've been through here. And remember, there's always a next time...**❞** DAVID

❝They're all heroes...❞ VICTORIA

WE CAN DO THIS...

Chapter Fifteen

What's In A Name?

"Victoria and I really wanted another baby. It was just a case of picking when to have one, because we're always so busy." **DAVID**

"I'm fine. Everything's fine. I'm continuing to work and have kept really active. Everything's seems pretty much the same as with the last pregnancy."

VICTORIA ANNOUNCES SHE IS PREGNANT FOR THE SECOND TIME.

"Anyone who's ever had kids knows the moment you have one – whether it's a son or a daughter – it's the best feeling in the world." DAVID

"Brooklyn's a very affectionate little boy, so he's going to be brilliant with the new baby. He's running about – kicking footballs, singing dancing. He's a big boy now." **DAVID**

"Brooklyn was the first person I told when the doctor confirmed I was pregnant. Then I sent him over to tell David the secret. David was practically in tears, he was so happy." VICTORIA

"Yes, Brooklyn is really looking forward to having a little brother or sister to play with." **VICTORIA**

POSH & **BECKS** *Talking*

"I can't wait for the new baby to be born."
SANDRA BECKHAM, DAVID'S MOTHER

"I love being pregnant. I like giving birth. Actually, I love it!" VICTORIA

"Victoria, you had a Caesarean. You didn't even feel it!" DAVID

"Overall, this has been a very exciting year for us. England are in the World Cup finals, Victoria's had her second Top Ten hit and now, we're expecting a new baby. It's fantastic." DAVID

"There are reasons I kept my pregnancy quiet for a while. First, I had to have a 12-week scan to know if everything was OK. The second reason was that I didn't want anyone to think I was releasing information to tie in with the release of my single, which was actually out a week before the announcement. Only my very close family knew."
VICTORIA RESPONDS TO CRITICS WHO ACCUSED HER OF USING HER PREGNANCY TO PROMOTE HER SECOND SOLO SINGLE, 'A MIND OF IT'S OWN'

"My mummy says I'm going to have a little sister called Paris."
BROOKLYN BECKHAM LETS SLIP ON THE SEX AND NAME OF DAVID AND VICTORIA'S BABY ON A VISIT TO MOTHERCARE.

"Victoria and David have decided they don't want to know the sex of the baby. And Brooklyn is still too young to know the difference. All he knows is he will have a brother... or a sister."
SPOKESPERSON FOR THE BECKHAMS

The Birth

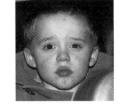

On Sunday, 1 September 2002 Victoria gave birth to a 7lb 4oz baby boy, Romeo, at Portland Hospital.

"Romeo's gorgeous and Victoria's great. She's sitting up in bed and all the family are here. The name? Romeo's just a name we love. We're both delighted." **DAVID**

"Yes, it's an unusual name. In that way, it's the same as Brooklyn. But it's David and Victoria's choice, so it's obviously what they wanted. But I know if Romeo turns out half as good as Brooklyn, he will be wonderful. I'm over the moon." TED BECKHAM, DAVID'S FATHER

"Romeo looks just like Brooklyn. He's got his nose and Victoria's chin. I was there when Romeo came out. It was awesome. Victoria and I might try and work on a five-a-side team in the next few months!" **DAVID**

"With David and I coaching, we'll have a good little side there..." TED BECKHAM

"Brooklyn came in just as Romeo was coming out. He's in awe of him." **DAVID**

"You're always nervous having children, but it's still the most beautiful thing in the world. Victoria is delighted." DAVID

"Victoria is, as you would expect, absolutely glowing." **SPOKESPERSON FOR PORTLAND HOSPITAL**

WHAT'S IN A NAME?

"I don't think Romeo's named after me, but if he is, I'm overwhelmed. I'd also like to wish the Beckhams 'Congratulations'. Nice choice of name, definitely. Actually, I reckon little Romeo will be a hit with the ladies with a name like that. Big up the Beckhams."

MC ROMEO, SO SOLID CREW

"Look, it's a name Victoria and David liked. I don't know if either of them studied 'Romeo and Juliet' at school..."

SPOKESPERSON FOR THE BECKHAMS

"Posh pips The Queen In Babycham's 'Celebrity Mother Of The Year' Poll"

HEADLINE, THE SCOTSMAN

"These days, Victoria Beckham is almost as famous for being a mum as she is for her music. She manages to balance a successful career with being a mother. It clear she loves her children and ordinary women admire that. I'm surprised the Queen came second, though. She's not someone often referred to when talking about famous mothers."

SPOKESPERSON FOR BABYCHAM

"Am I delighted about Romeo? You bet." VICTORIA